# It's Circle Time!

By
Elizabeth Flikkema

Cover Illustration by Robert Collier-Morales

Inside Illustrations by Janet Armbrust

Publisher
Carson-Dellosa Publishing Company, Inc.
Greensboro, North Carolina

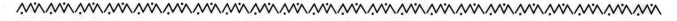

**Dedication**
To Brett William
who loves to explore new things.

**Credits:**
Author: Betsy Flikkema
Cover Artist: Robert Collier-Morales
Inside Illustrations: Janet Armbrust
Project Director: Sherrill B. Flora
Editor: Sharon Thompson, Sherrill B. Flora
Graphic Layout: Gray House Graphics

ISBN: 0-88724-915-9

# Table of Contents

# All About Me

## Building Language Experience

Talk about the differences and similarities among the children. Name an attribute, such as black hair, and have all the kids with that attribute do something, such as stand up, to identify themselves. Repeat with several different attributes: hair color, height, color of clothing, eye color, length of hair, hair style, gender, age, etc.

Pass out small mylar mirrors for students to look at themselves closely. Allow them to talk to each other about what they see in the mirror. Call attention to different things as they look. What colors do you see in your eyes? What direction are the hairs on your eyebrows going? Is the color of your skin the same on your face and hands? Do you have freckles? Can you count them? Does your eyelid cover part of your iris? Turn the lights down so children can see the size of their pupil change. Do you see your teeth when you smile? Are your lips shaped the same on the top and bottom? Side to side?

## Taking Turns

Paint a large face on a box. Cut holes for eyes and mouth. Play beanbag toss by tipping the box up and allowing students to toss a beanbag into the holes. Students cheer for each other as they play. Encourage team building, not competition.

Point to the different parts of your faces as you say this rhyme:
>Eye winker,
>Tom tinker (forehead),
>nose smeller,
>mouth eater,
>chin chopper, chin chopper,
>chin, chin, chin.

Touch the different parts of your body as you sing, "Head and Shoulders, Knees and Toes."
>Head and shoulders, knees and toes, knees and toes.
>Head and shoulders, knees and toes, knees and toes.
>Eyes and ears and mouth and nose.
>Head and shoulders, knees and toes, knees and toes.

## Literature

Read *We're Different, We're the Same* (Sesame Street Picturebacks) by Bobbi Jane Kates. Talk about what makes each one of us wonderful. Talk about the importance of differences in making the world a more interesting place. Copy page 5 for each student. Have the students draw pictures of themselves in the frame. They may include in the picture something they care about.

## Creative Movement

Have you ever heard the expression, "I'm all ears"? What does that mean? Give the children some expressions that use body parts and have them act them out literally and creatively. *Examples:* Hold yourself together. Put your nose to the grindstone. Keep your head on. Keep your eye on the ball. Hands down, big mouth, cold feet, butter fingers, etc.

**5**

∧∧∧∧∧∧∧∧∧∧∧∧∧∧∧∧∧∧∧∧∧∧∧∧∧∧∧∧∧∧∧∧∧∧∧∧∧

## Cognitive Skills Games . . . . . . . . . . . . . . . . . . . . . . . . . . . . . . . . . . . . . . . . . . . . . . . . . . . .

*Let's Count:* Have each child name a part of the body for the group to count. For example, you can count fingers, elbows, or eyes. (Students may count their own or you may count all the eyes in the group.)

***We're Different and the Same:*** Sit in the circle. Start with any child. That child must name one attribute that makes him or her different than the person on his/her right. Then, that child must name a different attribute that makes him or her different than the person on his/her right. Keep going around the circle. If the student names an attribute incorrectly or can't think of one, good naturedly send him or her to the center. When you say "switch," the students need to start naming attributes that make them the same as their neighbors. When you call "switch," the people in the center may raise their hands and get back into the game by naming something that makes them the same (or different) as someone in the circle. If they say it correctly, they may go sit by the person named.

*Body Riddles:* This game is like I spy, but you give clues about a specific part of the body and the children try to guess what it is. For example, I'm thinking of a part of the body that keeps your head warm and comes in different colors. What is it? (hair)

*Marching Body Match:* While you beat a rhythm instrument, the children march to the beat in a circle. When the beat stops, the teacher calls out a body part. The children need to turn to the person next to them and match that body part. For example, if the teacher calls out "knee," the children touch knees. You may have children do this to their right and left so no children are left out. Start the beat again and repeat with a different body part.

## Paying Attention . . . . . . . . . . . . . . . . . . . . . . . . . . . . . . . . . . . . . . . . . . . . . . . . . . . . . . . . . .

*Play Read My Lips:* Give the students directions without using your voice. They will have to really focus to figure out what you are saying. Give directions such as jump up and down, raise your hand, blink your eyes, and so on. After the game, discuss what made the game difficult. Talk about the importance of eye contact and speaking clearly when talking to others.

## Dismissal to the Next Activity . . . . . . . . . . . . . . . . . . . . . . . . . . . . . . . . . . . . . . . . . . . .

Dismiss students from circle time by naming attributes. For example, all the children with long hair may go to the

∧∧∧∧∧∧∧∧∧∧∧∧∧∧∧∧∧∧∧∧∧∧∧∧∧∧∧∧∧∧∧∧∧∧∧∧∧

# Animals (pets)

## Building Language Experience

Talk about what pets children have at home and how they take care of them. Have them tell about their personal responsibilities. What are the good things about having a certain pet? What are the difficult things? Have children share stories about getting a new pet and naming a pet. How did they choose the pets' names?

## Taking Turns

Duplicate page 8. Cut out the animals in advance. Give each child an animal picture. Taking turns around the circle, have each child tell what animal they have, what they will name the pet, and one thing the pet does, eats, or is good at.

## Literature

Read *The Berenstain Bears' Trouble With Pets* by Stan and Jan Berenstain. This book explores the positive and negative aspects of having a pet. Brother and Sister learn about taking responsibility.

Read *Bark, George* by Jules Feiffer. This hilariously illustrated book is about a puppy who can moo, quack, oink, and meow, but can't bark until the vet solves his unusual problem. This is a perfect story to act out with paper cutouts of the various animals and a large dog cutout with a hole for a mouth. (You pull the cat, pig, cow, and duck out of George's mouth.)

## Graphing Pets

You will need a long piece of butcher paper. Duplicate several copies of page 8. Cut out the animals in advance. Give each child a picture of the pet they have at home. If a child has two dogs and two mice, that child should have four pictures in total. Some children won't have any. Children who have more than one can be encouraged to share with them. Make a floor graph of the pets at our homes. Have all the children with dogs line up their pictures in a row. Then have all the children with mice, rats, gerbils, or hamsters put their pets in a line. Continue until all the pets are on the graph. Talk about the data. Which animal do we have the most? Which animal do we have the least? How many rabbits are there? Glue the pictures on the paper, label the graph, and hang it up in the hallway.

| DOGS | CATS | FISH | RODENTS | BIRDS | RABBITS |
|------|------|------|---------|-------|---------|
|  |  |  |  |  |  |
|  | 🐱 |  |  |  |  |
| 🐶 | 🐱 |  |  |  |  |
| 🐶 | 🐱 |  |  | 🐦 |  |
| 🐶 | 🐱 | 🐟 |  | 🐦 |  |
| 🐶 | 🐱 | 🐟 | 🐹 | 🐦 | 🐰 |

## Bring a Pet to School

Invite someone to bring a small pet, such as a rabbit, guinea pig, or a calm dog for show and tell. Have the children sit close in the circle so the pet can run in the circle and not get out. This is a wonderful experience for the children. Prepare the children in advance for how the pet may act. If they are surprised, they may jump away and let the pet out of the circle. Quiet voices will make the animal feel more comfortable so it will move around and explore.

## Creative Movement

Have the children perform the actions of an animal with the emotions you propose. For example, have them act like a sleepy cat, a happy butterfly, or a friendly dog. Play some classical music while the children are moving.

## Music

Sing "Mary Had a Little Lamb" or "BINGO" or "This Old Man."

### This Old Man

This old man, he played one.                    *(hold up one finger)*
He played knick-knack on my thumb        *(hold up thumb)*
With a knick-knack paddy-whack             *(roll hands around each other)*
Throw the dog a bone.                             *(pretend to throw)*
This old man went rolling home.              *(roll hands around each other)*

Verse two starts like this:
This old man, he played two.                   *(hold up two fingers)*
He played knick-knack on my shoe.          *(point to shoe)*
With a knick-knack . . .

Verse three starts like this:
This old man, he played three.                 *(hold up three fingers)*
He played knick-knack on my knee.          *(point to knee)*
With a knick-knack . . .

Verse four starts like this:
This old man, he played four.                   *(hold up four fingers)*
He played knick-knack on my door.          *(pretend to knock)*
With a knick-knack . . .

Verse five starts like this:
This old man, he played five.                    *(hold up five fingers)*
He played knick-knack on my hive.           *(follow a flying bee with your finger)*
With a knick-knack . . .

## Cognitive Skills Game

**Animal riddles:** Play this game like "I Spy." Either you or a student gives hints about an animal, while the rest of the class tries to guess what animal it is. For example, I am thinking of an animal that lives on a farm and gives milk. What is it? (a cow)

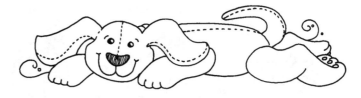

***Who has the puppy?:*** Children sit in a circle with one person in the center. The person in the center closes his or her eyes while the rest of the children pass a stuffed puppy (or gives another animal) behind their backs. When the center person barks (or other animal signal), whoever is holding the stuffed animal must hold it still. The center person must stay seated but looks around and has three guesses to figure out who has the puppy. If the person holding the puppy isn't found, he or she gets to go in the center.

*Active Game:* Play bird, bird, cat. Children sit in a circle. One person is the bird who walks (flies) around the outside of the circle. The bird says, "bird" as it touches each head. Whenever the bird chooses, it touches a head and says, "cat" instead of "bird." The cat jumps up and tries to catch the bird. While running, the bird says, "tweet" and the cat says, "meow." If the cat catches (tags) the bird, the bird goes into the center of the circle and the cat becomes the next bird. If the bird runs all the way around the circle, it sits down in the cat's place, and the cat becomes the next bird. The next time a bird goes into the center, the first bird goes back into the circle.

## Food

Make "people puppy chow" for a snack.
*Ingredients:*
3/4 cup smooth peanut butter
1 12-ounce bag of semi-sweet chocolate chips
1 stick margarine or butter
1 12-ounce box of corn or rice Chex cereal
2 1/2 cups powdered sugar
2 large paper grocery bags—one bag inside the other
Pour powdered sugar into the doubled grocery bags. Set aside. Empty the box of cereal into a large bowl. Set aside. In a saucepan, melt margarine, chocolate chips, and peanut butter, stirring constantly. When thoroughly melted, pour the mixture over the cereal and mix well to coat each piece. Immediately pour the cereal into the grocery bag and fold the top down twice. Shake and turn the bag several times until cereal is coated with sugar. Store in a large plastic bag when cool. Makes four quarts.

## Dismissal to Next Activity

Dismiss the students by the type of pet they have or don't have at home.

# Apples

## Building Language Experience . . . . . . . . . . . . . . . . . . . . . . . . . . . . . . . . . .

Bring in samples of different apples. The following apples have a variety of colors, shapes, and tastes: Granny Smith, Red Delicious, Yellow Delicious, Ida Red, Gala, and Jonathan. Pass the apples around the circle and talk about the names of the apples and compare the differences in appearance. Encourage the children to talk about how they like to eat apples: peeled and sliced, as applesauce, in pie, as juice, in cobbler, in muffins or cake, etc. Discuss how apples grow and what time of year they are ready to pick.

Talk to the children about handling the fruit gently. Demonstrate how bumping an apple causes a bruise. Observe the bruise over an hour and a day. On the next day, cut the apple to see the bruise from the inside.

## Taste Test . . . . . . . . . . . . . . . . . . . . . . . . . . . . . . . . . . . . . . . . . . . . .

Cut up three or four very different apples into bite-size pieces. Put the apples on paper plates. Number and label each apple and, if possible, put a whole apple of the same variety on each plate. Allow the children to taste the apples and describe the taste as best they can using language like sweet, sour, mild, sharp, strong, soft, and crisp. Write down the comments they make about each apple. There should be enough pieces that they can go back and taste one again to compare it with another. Encourage them to use comparative language rather than simply good and bad or like and dislike. After everyone has tasted the apples, talk about the words they used. Possibly come to a consensus about which apple was the sweetest, which was the most crisp, etc. Vote on the favorite apple and graph the favorites.

Taste apple juice and apple cider. Compare the taste, smell, and appearance. Pour the juice into small pitchers and let the children pour their own juice and cider into their cups.

## Literature. . . . . . . . . . . . . . . . . . . . . . . . . . . . . . . . . . . . . . . . . . . . . . .

Read about Johnny Appleseed. Also read *Ten Apples Up on Top!* by Dr. Seuss.

## Science . . . . . . . . . . . . . . . . . . . . . . . . . . . . . . . . . . . . . . . . . . . . . . . .

Cut an apple in half horizontally so you see a star pattern in the seeds. Show this to the students. (Cut another apple vertically to compare.) Tell the students that you are going to leave the cut apple on a paper plate overnight. Put one half face up and the other half face down on the plate. (For comparison, put the second cut apple in the refrigerator, in a plastic bag, or another place suggested by the children.) Ask the children what they think will happen to the apple over time. Write down their hypotheses. Observe the apple the next day. Ask the children to describe what happened. Compare what they say to what they said the day before. Why do they think the apple turned brown? Have they seen something like that before? When? Compare the different apple halves. Did any of the halves turn more or less brown? You may wish to extend this lesson if anyone proposes another way to preserve the apple (lemon juice).

## Finger Play . . . . . . . . . . . . . . . . . . . . . . . . . . . . . . . . . . . . . . . .

Way up high in the apple tree           *(point up)*
Grow three red apples 1, 2, 3.           *(count on fingers)*
I jumped for the apples,           *(jump and reach)*
And what did I get?           *(shrug and raise arms)*
One red apple just for me.           *(count one and point to self)*

Up in the tree were apples two.           *(point up and count to two)*
I jumped up but that wouldn't do.           *(jump and reach)*
I climbed a ladder           *(move hands alternately like climbing a ladder)*
And what did I get?           *(shrug and raise arms)*
One red apple just for you.           *(count one and point to someone else)*

Now I wanted to have some fun.           *(rub hands together)*
Up in the tree was apple one.           *(count on one finger)*
I shook that tree           *(pretend to shake tree)*
And what did I see?           *(shade eyes and look up)*
One red apple hanging in the sun.           *(make sun with arms and rock back and forth)*

〰〰〰〰〰〰〰〰〰〰〰〰〰〰〰〰〰〰〰〰〰〰〰〰〰〰〰〰〰〰〰

## Creative Movement

Have the children pretend they are apple trees. Their arms are branches. It is spring and there are pretty blossoms on the branches. The branches move lightly in the breeze. Now it is summer, and the summer sun is making the leaves grow, and the roots of the tree are taking in water. Tiny apples are growing on the branches. They aren't very heavy, but they weigh the branches down a little bit. As fall comes, the branches are getting full of big, ripe apples. The branches are bending down more and more as the heavy apples pull them down. Now it is time to pick the apples. The apples are gone from one branch, and it springs back up as light as a feather. The apples are gone from the other branch, and it springs back up light as a feather. Now the winter winds are coming. The branches sway lightly until the tree goes quietly to sleep and dreams about the next spring.

## Cognitive Skills Game

**Apple Count:** Sit in a circle and give an apple to one child. That child chooses a number to which the group will count. As he or she passes the apple to the person on his or her left, the first person says, "one." The apple passes from person to person as the counting continues. When the counting gets to the number the first person named, the apple stops. Now the person holding the apple gets to choose the number of times the apple will be passed. Continue this and practice counting. Set the number range according to the class's ability.

**Counting:** Bring in a basket of 5–10 apples. Ask the children to estimate how many apples they think are in the basket. Count the apples together as you take them out of the basket. Ask the children if they think the apples will fit in another container that you show them. Try it. Count the apples as you put them in the next container. Repeat with other containers of different sizes and shapes.

## Field Trip

Visit an apple orchard. It is best if the children can see the orchard at picking time. They will be able to see the different kinds of trees, as well as the picking and packing methods of the orchard. Ask the farmer where the apples will be shipped and how they will get there. Notice how the branches bend low under the weight of the apples. If possible, observe a cider press and taste the cider. Look for bees and talk about the job of a bee at an apple orchard.

## Painting

Have the children paint a red, green, and/or yellow apple at the easel. Add a brown stem with a marker after the paint has dried.

〰〰〰〰〰〰〰〰〰〰〰〰〰〰〰〰〰〰〰〰〰〰〰〰〰〰〰〰〰〰 Apples 〰

# Beaches

## Building Language Experience

While the children are gathered, unpack a beach bag and set up as if you are at the beach (towel, sunscreen, sunglasses, book, water to drink, pail and shovel, swim toy, etc.). Talk with the children about what you are doing. Listen to their comments about the experience of going to the beach. This is especially nice to do on a cold winter day. Allow the children to talk about what they like to do at the beach. What toys do they bring? Do they know how to swim? Have they ever had a sunburn?

## Senses

Pass around a conch shell for students to listen to the sound.
Pass around shells or other ocean finds that have a smell of the ocean about them.
In a shallow pan of sand, let each student use a finger to draw the letter of the day, their name, or a shape.
Allow the students to taste salty water.
Look at pictures of the beach.
Have students close their eyes and listen to ocean sounds from a relaxation CD.

## Literature

Read *Beach Play* by Marsha Hayles. This delightful book will give students a sense of being there on the beach. The illustrations are adorable, and the language is simple.

## Counting Rhyme

Teach the children the following rhyme. Give them a half-sheet of light brown paper and five shells or crab cutouts to move as you say the rhyme together.

Five little crabs playing on the shore.
One skittered off and then there were four.
Four little crabs feeling rather free.
One saw a snack and then there were three.
Three little crabs wondered what to do.
One caught a wave and then there were two.
Two little crabs basking in the sun.
One got too hot and then there was one.
One little crab feeling all alone,
Slipped in the water and all the crabs were home.

See page 15 for crab pattern.

## Movement

Teach students to walk like crabs. First they sit down on the floor and lean back on their hands. Then they lift their bottoms off the ground with their tummies face up. They walk head-first with their hands and feet. After a little practice, you can have crab races in an open space.

Have children pretend to be seagulls flying gracefully over the beach. They can fly with graceful wings or soar and turn circles. Then they can swoop down and pick up something to eat. Or they can pretend to be ducks floating on the water with their wings tucked in at their sides. Sometimes they dive down to get something to eat. Sometimes they waddle on the shore.

# Crab Pattern

Directions found on page 14.

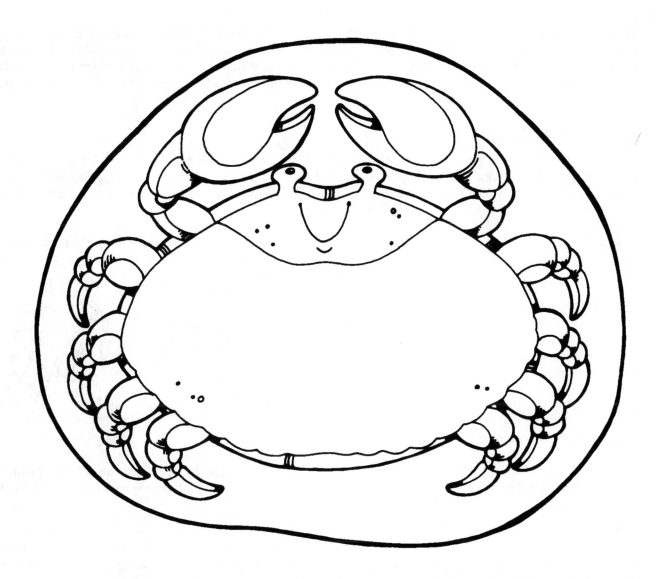

ᄿᄿᄿᄿᄿᄿᄿᄿᄿᄿᄿᄿᄿᄿᄿᄿᄿᄿᄿᄿᄿᄿᄿᄿᄿᄿᄿᄿᄿᄿᄿ

## Cognitive Skills

***Shell Sort:*** Bring in a variety of shells of different sizes, colors, and shapes. Put the shells in the center of the circle and talk about what they look like. Ask the children to suggest ways to sort the shells. Write the sorting words on index cards. Make two circles from 6 inches or 2 meter pieces of yarn. Choose two index cards and put one card in each circle. Have the children take turns putting a shell in the correct circle. For example, one circle may be for brown shells. Another circle may be for swirly shells. When a shell can fit in either circle, let the children problem-solve about where to put it.

***Watch Carefully:*** Pick out six very different shells and put them on a tray or plate. Look at the shells together and talk about what they look like. Cover the shells with a cloth and secretly take away one shell. Uncover the shells and ask the children to describe the shell that is missing. When they can tell you which one is missing, show it to them and put it back on the plate. Cover the shells again and secretly remove a different shell. Repeat the game.

## Creative Dramatics

Set the tone for sitting by the seashore. Allow the children to sway with the breeze and whoosh with the waves and react to the hot sun and sand. Tell the students that a breeze is blowing. The waves are rolling in. The sun is shining, and the sand is hot under your feet. We are at the seashore, and someone is selling seashells. You can hear her/him calling "Seashells for Sale! Seven cents a shell!"

Give a bucket of shells to one student and ask him or her to repeat the line, "Seashells for Sale! Seven cents a shell!" Have all the children but the seller sit down. You may prepare a sign in advance that says, "7¢ a shell" Have the students say the tongue twister. "She/He sells seashells by the seashore."

Then the child shouts out the sales call. "Seashells for Sale! Seven cents a shell!"

Give seven pennies to another student who can "buy" a seashell from the seller.

You can allow the students to take turns being the seller and buyer in circle time and then put the shells (and some pennies) in a play area for center time.

Have a beach picnic: Tell the children to bring in beach towels for the special day. They can eat their picnic on their own towels. Have parents help you by providing some special treats: blue gelatin with gummy sharks, hot dogs, chips, lemonade, and watermelon, if available.

## Art

Use sand like glitter. Have students draw a beach scene on heavy paper. Then they use a cotton swab to put glue wherever they want sand. Sprinkle sand on the glue and shake the excess off into a tub.

***Painting:*** Have the children paint a large sun with yellow paint at the easel. Remind them that the sun is a circle with rays coming out from all sides.

## Sensory Table

Put sand in the sensory table with shovels, small pails, and lots of containers for filling, sifting, and pouring. Put water in a large tub with towels all around. Fill the tub with floating and sinking toys.

ᄿᄿᄿᄿᄿᄿᄿᄿᄿᄿᄿᄿᄿᄿᄿᄿᄿᄿᄿᄿᄿᄿᄿᄿᄿᄿᄿᄿᄿᄿᄿ

# Birds

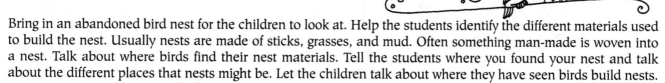

## Building Language Experience . . . . . . . . . . . . . . . . . . . . . . . . .

If you have a birdfeeder at home (or school) talk about what kinds of birds you see there. Look at pictures of different kinds of birds from backyard birds to flamingos, penguins, and ostriches. Discuss the features of a variety of birds from the smallest to the largest. Let the children talk about their experiences with seeing and hearing birds.

Bring in an abandoned bird nest for the children to look at. Help the students identify the different materials used to build the nest. Usually nests are made of sticks, grasses, and mud. Often something man-made is woven into a nest. Talk about where birds find their nest materials. Tell the students where you found your nest and talk about the different places that nests might be. Let the children talk about where they have seen birds build nests.

## Exploring the Senses . . . . . . . . . . . . . . . . . . . . . . . . . . . . . . . . .

Children are already familiar with many bird sounds: hoot of an owl, caw of a crow, quack of a duck, peep of a chick, and probably the sounds of some regional backyard birds. You can name a bird (or hold up a picture) and ask the students to make the bird sound, or you can make the sounds and ask the students to name (or point to) the birds.

Teach the children American Sign Language for bird. Make a V with your index and middle finger. Then open and close it like a beak in front of your mouth.

## Literature . . . . . . . . . . . . . . . . . . . . . . . . . . . . . . . . . . . . . . . . . .

Read *Little Bird, Biddle Bird* by David Kirk. This story about a baby bird finding its first meal is by the same author as *Miss Spider*. The colors are bright and playful, and the text is simple and rhyming.

*Birds, Nests and Eggs: Take-Along Guide* by Mel Boring is a nice resource for your classroom. The pictures are beautiful, and it is full of interesting facts and information written at a young child's interest level.

## Finger Play . . . . . . . . . . . . . . . . . . . . . . . . . . . . . . . . . . . . . . . . . .

Cut out five birds from felt or construction paper. (Use patterns on page 18.) Act out the story with the cutouts. If you use felt, cut out a felt tree with five branches. Alternatively, use a brown glove as a tree. Put a piece of tape on each bird, and stick the birds to the tips of the glove fingers.

*Remove the birds as you tell the story:*
Five little birds on a tree in the spring
One little bird flew off to sing.
The second little bird spotted a treat.
Bird number three hopped off—tweet, tweet.
The fourth little bird spotted its home.
The fifth bird was there all alone.
Five little birds on a lovely day
All came back to the tree to play.

# Five Little Birds

Directions found on page 17.

Directions found on page 19.

CD-0206 *It's Circle Time!*

ᴧᴠᴧᴠᴧᴠᴧᴠᴧᴠᴧᴠᴧᴠᴧᴠᴧᴠᴧᴠᴧᴠᴧᴠᴧᴠᴧᴠᴧᴠᴧᴠᴧᴠᴧᴠᴧᴠᴧᴠᴧᴠᴧᴠᴧᴠ

## Music and Movement . . . . . . . . . . . . . . . . . . . . . . . . . . . . .

Give the children streamers, feathers, and scarves. Play music that is lively, while the children imagine they are some kind of bird. They dance to the music, waving their feathers, streamers and scarves. There is not one right way to dance like a bird. They may all dance like the same kind of bird or each dance like a different bird of their choosing.

## Cognitive Skills . . . . . . . . . . . . . . . . . . . . . . . . . . . . . . . . . .

*Sound Patterns:* Make up a sound pattern using bird calls. For example, tweet, caw, caw, tweet, caw, caw. You may use finger plays along with the sounds. For tweet, wave your hands like wings. For caw, make an opening and closing beak with your hands by your mouth. Repeat the pattern a couple times and then have the students join you.

*Nests and Counting:* Use paper muffin cups as nests. Write a numeral on the inside bottom of each nest. Use jellybeans as eggs. Have the children take turns counting the correct number of jellybean eggs into each nest.

*Counting Feathers:* Make a bird body out of play dough (a round ball shape). Push a paper bird's head (make a copy of the pattern on page 18) into one side of the bird body. The children will count and put feathers (available in craft stores) into the opposite side of the bird body for the tail. Show a number card and have the children take turns putting the correct number of tail feathers into the bird body. To involve more children at a time, prepare three birds out of play dough. Three children at a time can count and add feathers. Compare the number of feathers in each. Then choose a different number and three other children to count feathers. To make this a center activity, duplicate several bird heads on different colors of construction paper and write the numerals on the bird heads. The children can change the heads and feathers to make different birds.

## Games . . . . . . . . . . . . . . . . . . . . . . . . . . . . . . . . . . . . . . .

*Finch, Finch, Blue Jay:* Blue jays are aggressive birds at the feeder. When they come around, the other birds seem to scatter. The children sit in a circle, forming a bird feeder for this game. One child is "it" and walks around the outside of the circle. "It" may tap two people on the head and say "finch." Those finches stand up in the center of the circle and wait until the person who is "it" chooses the blue jay. When the blue jay is tapped on the head, he or she stands up and tries to shoo away the finches. The finches must run out of the circle, run around the outside of the circle, and try to sit down in an empty spot before the blue jay can tag them. Whoever is tagged is the next "it." If no one is tagged, the blue jay becomes "it."

*Feather Painting:* Choose a bright color of paint for this texture art. Pour a thin layer of paint on a paper plate. The children dip the side of a feather (available at craft stores) in the paint and then paint on paper with the feather. They can explore how different movements of the feather create different textures. You will probably need a feather for each child because when they get drenched with paint, the feathers lose their interesting textures.

ᴧᴠᴧᴠᴧᴠᴧᴠᴧᴠᴧᴠᴧᴠᴧᴠᴧᴠᴧᴠᴧᴠᴧᴠᴧᴠᴧᴠᴧᴠᴧᴠᴧᴠᴧᴠᴧᴠᴧᴠᴧᴠᴧᴠᴧᴠ

 CD-0206 *It's Circle Time!*

# Birthdays

## Building Language Experience

While seated in a circle, show the children a wrapped package with a bow. Ask them when and why we get presents. What are some of their favorite presents they have received? Talk about what is on the wrapping paper, as well as how it is wrapped and decorated. Why are presents so pretty? Why do we wrap presents? They may wish to guess what is inside. (You may place a stuffed animal or toy inside.) Unwrap it in front of the class. Show the children how to unwrap without ripping the paper. Encourage them to recycle wrapping paper.

Talk about birthdays. As you say the months of the year, have students stand up when you name their birthday month. Talk about how old each student is. Talk about what makes a birthday special. Have the children share what their family does for birthdays. Do they go somewhere? Do they have a special song? Do they have special foods?

Sing the "Happy Birthday" song. If it isn't anyone's birthday, sing to a classroom stuffed animal, to the earth, the school, or anything else that is appropriate.

## Literature

Read *McDuff's Birthday* by Rosemary Wells. Wells' McDuff is a wonderful character.

Read *The Secret Birthday Message* by Eric Carle. In this story, Tim follows clues to find his birthday surprise.

## Creative Movement/Gross Motor

*Candle Flames:* Have the children pretend to be stiff, straight birthday candles with flickering flames on top (arms overhead). When you pretend to blow them out, they bring their hands down at their sides. Pick out the children who can stand the straightest to blow out the candles next time.

*Candle Jump:* Tape 10" (25 cm) long paper candles to the floor far enough apart that children aren't jumping into each other. As you recite the nursery rhyme "Jack Be Nimble," have the children jump over their own candles.

> Jack be nimble,
> Jack be quick,
> Jack jump over the candlestick.
> It was quite a jump he did make
> To jump right over his birthday cake.

## Music

Put a large box in the center of the circle. Have one child climb inside out of view, but don't close the top. Have the other children sing a song and clap in rhythm. At the end of the song, the child bursts up out of the box and sings the last line with the others.

*Song:* Sing to the tune of "Pop, goes the Weasel."

> We'll sing a birthday song for you.
> How old are you today?
> We love the cake and presents, too.
> Surprise, it's your birthday!

## Cognitive Skills

**Patterns:** Use two or three different wrapping papers with simple designs for a pattern activity. Cut out several squares from each wrapping paper and glue the squares on stiff paper (the paper can be larger than the wrapping paper). Have four to six children stand up where everyone in the circle can see them. Make a visual pattern by giving them each a wrapping paper square. For example, give the first child striped paper, the second child red paper, the third child striped paper, and the fourth child red paper. Ask the children to help you name the designs (or colors) and then "read the pattern" to you. Ask them to tell you what design (color) will come next. Whoever names the next design can stand up and continue the pattern by holding the correct wrapping paper square. Repeat with other patterns of different complexities (depending on experience with patterns).

## Center Activities

**Play Dough:** Have the children make play dough cakes and put birthday candles in the cakes.

**Wrapping Presents:** Put out recycled wrapping paper (from the unwrapping game), newspaper, or tissue paper, along with tape and shoe boxes for children to wrap.

**Hat Factory:** Decorate cone-shaped, paper birthday hats by gluing on paper designs, flower shapes, sequins, feathers, and other recycled pieces.

## Game

In advance, wrap a box with several layers of inexpensive wrapping paper *(one wrap for each child in the class). Pass the wrapped box around the circle as you play music. When the music stops, the person holding the box unwraps one layer of wrapping paper. (Encourage them to unwrap carefully so you can reuse the paper during free time at a wrapping center.) When the student is done unwrapping, start the music again. So that everyone gets a chance to unwrap, the children who have already unwrapped should move back out of the circle. The circle will get smaller and smaller as the game continues.

*Duplicate the mini-book on page 22. Put one mini-book in each layer of the wrapping. When children have unwrapped a layer, they many read (and color) their mini-book.

Happy birthday to you!
3

Pin the tail on the donkey.
2

What is in the box?
4

It is time for a birthday party.
1

# Dinosaurs

## Building Language Experience ........................................

Find out what children already know and think about dinosaurs. Do they think all dinosaurs were big? Do they know that some dinosaurs ate meat and some ate plants? Do they know that they lived long ago and that people didn't live on the earth until about 60 million years after the dinosaurs were gone? What do they know about the meaning of "extinct?" Enjoy a conversation about dinosaurs and be prepared for questions and inaccurate facts. There are many great books about dinosaurs. It may be helpful to have a dinosaur encyclopedia on hand with pictures and answers to questions.

## Literature ........................................

Read *How Big Were the Dinosaurs* by Bernard Most. This book compares the sizes of different dinosaurs to familiar objects to children. Some dinosaurs were huge, but some were very small.

Read *Patrick's Dinosaurs* by Carol Carrick. In this story, Patrick imagines the dinosaurs his brother describes to him living right in our world. The story weaves facts and imagination very nicely.

Have the class vote on a dinosaur to measure. Look up how long the dinosaur might have been from head to tail and cut a piece of yarn that long. Then, have the children go outside or in the hallway to hold the yarn and stretch it to its full length. As children are standing at different points along the yarn, tell them where on the dinosaur each might be standing. For example, Tanya is standing at the dinosaur's shoulder.

## Creative Movement ........................................

After looking at pictures and talking about different kinds of dinosaurs, it is time to act like dinosaurs. Play music and allow the children to move like dinosaurs around the circle. Encourage each child to pick a certain kind of dinosaur to mimic. A tyrannosaurus might move very differently from a flying dinosaur or an apatosaurus.

## Cognitive Skills ........................................

Teach the children American Sign Language for *dinosaur*. Bend three fingers on each hand (like claws) in front of your chest and move them alternately up and down two times.

***Dinosaur Color:*** Duplicate the large dinosaur pattern on page 25 on three different colors of paper. Make at least three of each color. Since no people lived when dinosaurs were around, we have no idea what color they might have been. (Isn't there a nice lesson there about skin color?) Have four to six children hold the colored dinosaurs in a pattern for the rest of the group to see. "Read the pattern" with the class and ask someone to tell you what color dinosaur comes next. Ask other children to stand up and hold colored dinosaurs to continue the pattern.

***Counting:*** Duplicate fifty-five small dinosaurs (patterns on page 24) on brightly colored paper. On 8" x 10" cards, write a numeral (from 1 to 10) and glue that many dinosaurs on the card. Use these cards to practice number recognition. Show a card and ask the children to tell you how many dinosaurs there are.

MMMMMMMMMMMMMMMMMMMMMMMMM

## Music

Where Have the Dinosaurs Gone?
Sing to the tune of "Oh Where Has My Little Dog Gone?"

    Oh where, oh where have the dinosaurs gone?
    Oh where, oh where can they be?
    With their teeth so sharp and their tails so strong
    Oh why couldn't they stay to meet me?

### Counting Song

Cut nine little dinosaurs out of felt for the children to count while they sing. Sing to the tune of "Ten Little Indians."

    One hungry, two hungry, three hungry stegosaurs.
    Four hungry, five hungry, six hungry stegosaurs.
    Seven hungry, eight hungry, nine hungry stegosaurs.
    Eating grass and leaves.

*Other verses:* hungry raptors—hunting down their prey; hungry dinosaurs—living long ago; tall dinosaurs—eating from the trees; tiny dinosaurs—running fast and free; giant dinosaurs—stomping through the swamp.

## Art

***Dinosaur Textures:*** Duplicate the large dinosaur pattern on page 25 for each child. Provide a variety of textured surfaces for them to put under their dinosaur shape and make a crayon rubbing.

***Crayon Resist:*** Paleontologists learn about dinosaurs by studying their bones. Duplicate the large dinosaur pattern for each child. First, have students draw bones on the dinosaur with a white crayon. Then, have them paint over the crayon with any color of paint. The crayon bones will show through the paint.

## Sensory Table

***Paleontology:*** Fill the sensory table/tub with sand and plastic dinosaurs. Put some dinosaurs in plastic eggs and some inside balls of clay or play dough. Also provide small tools for digging (spoons), scraping (plastic knives), and sweeping (paintbrushes).

## Dismissal to the Next Activity

Dismiss children by naming different dinosaurs. Students may walk to their next activity when you name their favorite. Encourage them to walk like a dinosaur.

### Dinosaur Patterns
Directions found on page 23.

MMMMMMMMMMMMMMMMMMMMMMMMM

# Large Dinosaur Pattern

Directions found on page 23.

# Directional Words

## (up and down, over, under, front, back, etc.)

### Building Language Experience

Ask the children to name things that are UP. Talk about different ways that things can be up (leaves in the trees, airplanes, lights on the ceiling, upstairs, top of the page, and so on). Ask the children to name things that are DOWN. Talk about how things can be down (under the ground, feet, feelings, bottom of a page, and so on.)

Have a discussion about good hiding places at their houses or neighborhood. As the children talk about their wonderful hiding places, repeat and emphasize the directional words they use. They will use words such as behind, under, next to, and in. Tell them that these words help us describe where to go or where something is. Show them the cards on page 28 and talk about the directional words illustrated there.

### Finger Plays

Wee Willie Winkie runs through the town
    *(finger and thumb make "wee;" then index and middle finger make running motion)*
Upstairs and downstairs in his nightgown     *(point up; point down)*
Knocking at the windows, calling through the locks,     *(knocking motion; cup hands around mouth)*
"Are the children all in bed? For now it's eight o'clock."     *(rest cheek on hands; look at watch)*

Hickory, Dickory Dock.     *(fist over fist)*
The mouse ran up the clock.     *(fingers run up your arm)*
The clock struck one.     *(hold up one finger)*
The mouse ran down.     *(fingers run down your arm)*
Hickory, Dickory Dock.     *(fist over fist)*

### Game

***Obstacle Course:*** Duplicate page 28 and cut out the cards. Put the cards by obstacles throughout the room so the children know what they need to do at each station. Tell the children that they are going to follow a course and do what the directions tell them to do. For example, they may go through a tunnel, under a table, over a chair, up a climber, down a slide, next to a brick wall, across a strip of tape, and around a puppet stage. You may want to use this game with the book, *We're Going on a Bear Hunt.*

***Simon Says:*** Play Simon Says with the traditional rules, but have Simon use directional words. Simon may use the cards on page 28 as cues. For example, put your thumb UNDER your chin, put your hands AROUND your body. If Simon gives a direction without saying "Simon says" first, then whoever follows the direction becomes the new Simon.

***Hide and Seek:*** Play hide and seek in the classroom. Have one to four children step out of the room while the rest of the children hide. When everyone is hidden, invite the children back into the room to find the hidden ones. As children are found, they come back to the circle to wait until everyone is found. The first children found will be the next ones to seek.

## Music and Movement

***Up and Down:*** Purchase a slide whistle at a toy store. This is a simple recorder with a bar that you pull and push in the body of the instrument. Rather than placing your fingers over holes, you move the bar up and down to create different notes. It is inexpensive and creates a fun sliding sound. Show the children how you make the different sounds. Then tell them that they are going to move with the music. As the pitch of the whistle goes up, they slowly stand up. As the whistle goes down in pitch, they slowly sit down. You can slide the pitch up and down slowly or quickly. You can make it go down or up a little or a long way. This is a very fun activity as the children move up and down with the music. It's a great listening activity.

***Shake Around:*** Give each child a shaker. (Put sand, rice, dried beans, or pasta in plastic eggs, egg cartons, small boxes, or empty soda pop bottles. Tape the container tightly before shaking.) While you play music, tell the children where to shake using directional words. For example, shake over your head, under your arm, next to your ear, between your knees, etc.

## Science

***Temperature:*** You will need a thermometer to measure water temperature. Be sure that it is not a mercury thermometer. Prepare a cup of hot water and a glass of ice water in advance. Then while the children watch, put the thermometer in the hot water and make sure they can all see the red line climb UP. Put the thermometer in the cold water so they can see the red line go DOWN. Move the thermometer back and forth between hot and cold to reinforce the concept that hot water makes the temperature go up, and cold water makes the temperature go down. Talk about the weather outside in terms of whether the temperature will go up or down.

***Under the Ground:*** Talk about what is UNDER the ground in different places. In the soil of a garden, you will find roots, worms, bulbs, seeds, and insects. If possible, collect some soil from a garden in a clear container. Plant some seeds and watch the changes underground. Some animals live underground. Under a house, there is a basement. Under a city, there may be subways and pipes. Encourage the children to think about what is under their feet.

# Following Direction Cards

Directions found on page 26.

# Eggs

## Building Language Experience

Put small plastic dinosaurs in plastic (Easter) eggs and bring them to circle time in an egg carton. Open the carton in front of the children and tell them that chickens aren't the only animals that lay eggs. Tell them that you have some eggs here that are ready to hatch. I wonder what kind of animal will be hatching? Do you think it could be a . . . As you make suggestions, have the children guess whether it could be that and offer reasons why it couldn't be that. Encourage them to ask questions about the animals inside the eggs. You may pass the eggs around and let the children handle them (carefully). Tell the children that you hear something; it must be the animals trying to get out of the shells. Ask the children to help the animals break out of their shells. When they see that they are dinosaurs, talk about dinosaur facts. Let the children share what they know. Dinosaurs hatched from eggs just like reptiles today hatch from eggs.

Alternatively, put different animals in the plastic eggs: birds, snakes, frogs, turtles, fish, bugs, dinosaurs, and other "oviparous" animals. When the children open the eggs, talk about the different animals that come from eggs.

## Literature

Read *Chickens Aren't the Only Ones* by Ruth Heller. This book tells about the different animals that hatch from eggs.

## Creative Movement/Reflecting

Have the children curl up in a ball and pretend they are in a shell. Ask them to imagine what it is like inside the shell. What do they feel, see, and hear? Then ask them to imagine they have a special tool on their mouth called an egg tooth that will help them to peck their way out of a shell and hatch. Then ask each child in turn to act like an animal that comes from an egg. The other children can guess what animal they are.

## Sensory Exploration

Ask the children to close their eyes and keep them closed as you move around the circle and tickle each child in the face with a feather. Hide the feather and let them open their eyes and talk about what happened. Pass feathers around for children to feel and look at closely. Provide magnifying glasses for children to observe even more closely.

## Motor Skills

Use hard-boiled eggs or plastic eggs with a little bit of water inside for this coordination activity. Divide the class into two groups. Put two strips of masking tape on the floor parallel to each other. Give a spoon and an egg to each team. One by one the children have to balance the egg on the spoon as they walk heel to toe along the tape strip. If someone drops an egg, he or she must go back to the beginning of the tape strip and try again. You can divide the teams in half so the players pass the egg and spoon to the next player at the end of the tape, or keep the teams whole so a player must walk across and back before passing off the egg and spoon.

## Graphing Activity

Ask the children to name different ways to eat eggs: fried, scrambled, boiled, in quiche, etc. Write down the different ways on index cards with a simple sketch next to the word. Put the cards on a floor graph. Give each child a plastic egg, and ask them to choose their favorite way to eat their eggs. Then, have them put their plastic eggs on the floor graph. When all the eggs are in place, talk about the data with questions such as the following: Which way of eating eggs is most popular? Which way is least popular? How many more/fewer people like scrambled than fried?

## Cognitive Skills Games

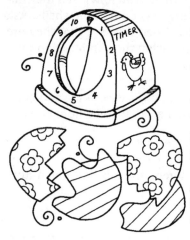

*How Long?* Use an egg timer (usually a three-minute timer with sand, but one-minute timers are available) to time different activities. Can you sing a favorite song or read a book before the timer is done? Can you hop around the room? How many times can you pass an object around the circle in the allotted time? Try different things to gain a sense of how long a minute (or three minutes) is.

*Who Has the Egg?* Children take turns sitting in the center of the circle. Recite "Humpty Dumpty" while the children pass an egg around the circle behind their backs. The person in the center has to guess who is holding the egg when the rhyme is done.

*Matching Designs:* Cut out large egg shapes from different wallpaper samples. Cut each egg shape in half with a zig-zag or swirly cut. Pass out the halves in the circle and allow the children with matching halves to find each other.

## Food

Read *Green Eggs and Ham* by Dr. Seuss. Make green eggs and ham by adding a little green food coloring to scrambled eggs and adding cooked, diced ham. As you pass out the samples, use words from the book to ask the children if they will try green eggs and ham. Encourage the children to politely accept the green eggs and ham using a rhyming word. For example: Will you try them with a mouse? I will try them in a house. Will you try them on a train? I will try them in the rain.

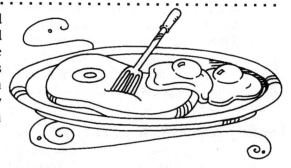

## Painting

Give children two or three colors at the easel. Tell them to draw a large oval shape for an egg and fill it in with a pattern of colors and designs.

# Families

## Building Language Experience . . . . . . . . . . . . . . . . . . . . . . . . . . . . . . . . . . . . . .

Bring a picture of your own family to the circle and tell the children who is in your family. Talk about names, ages, and family activities. Then ask the children to talk about their families. You may lead the discussion by asking children questions such as, "Raise your hand if you are the oldest child in your family." Guide the children to discover that families come in many different configurations. A family is a group of people who live together and care about (and for) each other.

*Think, Pair, Share:* Ask the children to think of one thing they like about their family. (e.g., My family plays games on Friday nights.) Give them a minute of thinking time. Then ask them to turn to a neighbor and tell that one thing to that child. When everyone has paired and talked with a neighbor, take turns around the circle and listen to each child's statement about his or her family.*

*If possible, write down each statement on a separate paper. At free time the children can draw a family picture on the paper with their statement on it. Gather all the papers together in a class book. Read the finished book to the class and send it home with each child one at a time.

Read *The Relatives Came* by Cynthia Rylant. This warm and funny book has beautiful language and fun pictures. The relatives come from Virginia to stay for a while, and the families really enjoy each other's company. Talk about relatives: cousins, grandparents, aunts and uncles, etc. Allow the children to tell stories about their relatives.

Encourage the children to bring family pictures from home. Pass the picture around the circle and allow the child to tell about the picture. Hang the pictures on a bulletin board that the children can see up close. Label the pictures with the last name (Wilson family).

## Cognitive Skills . . . . . . . . . . . . . . . . . . . . . . . . . . . . . . . . . . . . . . . . . . . . . . . .

Teach the American Sign Language for *family*: Make the letter f with both hands—index finger and thumb make a circle—with fingertips touching. Circle the fs around and bring them together again.

*Last Names:* Ask one child at a time to tell his or her last name. Talk about what letter the last name begins with. Clap out the syllables of the last name on your lap and have the children repeat the name with you as they also clap on their laps. Encourage the children to notice when two last names have the same beginning sound or the same number of beats.

*Let's Count:* In this game, students will stand up if you name a family attribute that fits them. Then the group counts the number of standing children. After counting, those children sit down, and you name another attribute. *Examples:* "Stand up if you have two brothers." "Stand up if you live in an apartment." Stand up if your dad reads to you before bed."

## Creative Movement Game

***Play Mom or Dad Says:*** Like Simon Says, one child gives directions for the rest of the class to follow. The directions can be family/home related, such as "Mom says, make your bed." The other children pretend to do what Mom says. But if the direction is not preceded by "Mom (or Dad) says," then they should not do it. If a child does not follow the directions, he or she becomes Mom or Dad.

***Who's the Parent?*** Have one child sit in the center of the circle and close his or her eyes while you silently point to one child who will be the "parent." The parent will lead the kids in the circle in some kind of action. All the children do the same action. It is the job of the person in the center to figure out who is the parent. For example, the parent will start clapping or stomping or turning circles. All the "children" will do the same thing until they see that the leader has changed actions. The children and parent will try to be discreet so it is not obvious who is starting the action. Without warning, the parent will change action and all the others will quickly do the same. The person in the center will watch for clues and guess who is leading. When he or she guesses correctly, he or she joins the circle and a new center person is chosen.

## Music

Sing to the tune of BINGO.

> I love my family, they're the best.
> My daddy is a great one.
> D-A-D-D-Y D-A-D-D-Y D-A-D-D-Y
> And daddy is his name-O.
> I love my family, they're the best.
> My mommy is a great one.
> M-O-M-M-Y M-O-M-M-Y M-O-M-M-Y
> And mommy is her name-O.

The children may like to change the adjectives from great to kind, fun, sweet, smart, big, old, and so on.

## Finger Play

| | |
|---|---|
| Some families are large. | *(hold hands far apart with palms facing)* |
| Some families are small, | *(hold palms close together)* |
| But I love my family best of all! | *(hug self)* |

## Painting

Have the children paint a house by making a square base and a triangle top. They can add a sun and some trees. When that has dried, they can add details to the house with markers.

## Dismissal to the Next Activity

Dismiss students from circle time by naming attributes they have in common with their parents. For example, you may go if you have the same eye color as your mom.

# Farms

## Building Language Experience . . . . . . . . . . . . . . . . . . . . . . . . . . . . .

Put a real farm tool in the center of the circle and talk about what it is used for. Ask the children to name the animals and things that they can find on a farm. Copy and color the picture of a barn (pattern on page 34) in advance and place it where children can see it. Ask the children what things they might find in a barn. They may name animals, farm equipment, and crops.

Tell the children that there are different kinds of farms. Farms provide the grocery stores with the food we buy: milk, vegetables, fruit, meat, and grains that are used for bread. Show each picture and put it by the barn as you talk about the different farm products. (Patterns on page 35.)

## Music . . . . . . . . . . . . . . . . . . . . . . . . . . . . . . . . . . . . . . . . . . . .

Sing "Old Mac Donald Had a Farm."

Sing "Oats and Beans and Barley Grow."
> Oats and beans and barley grow.
> Oats and beans and barley grow .
> Do you or I or anyone know how oats and beans and barley grow?
> First the farmer sows his seeds,
> Then he stands and takes his ease,
> Stamps his feet and claps his hands and turns around to view his land.

***Animals Around the Farm***: Sing to the tune of "The Wheels on the Bus." Children move around and act like the animal as they sing.
> The cow in the barn goes moo, moo, moo,
> Moo, moo, moo, moo, moo, moo.
> The cow in the barn goes moo, moo, moo,
> All around the farm.
> The duck in the pond goes quack, quack, quack.
> The pig in the mud goes oink.
> The hen in the coop goes cluck.
> The sheep in the hay goes baa.

# Farm Patterns

Directions found on page 33.

# Farm Patterns

Directions found on page 33.

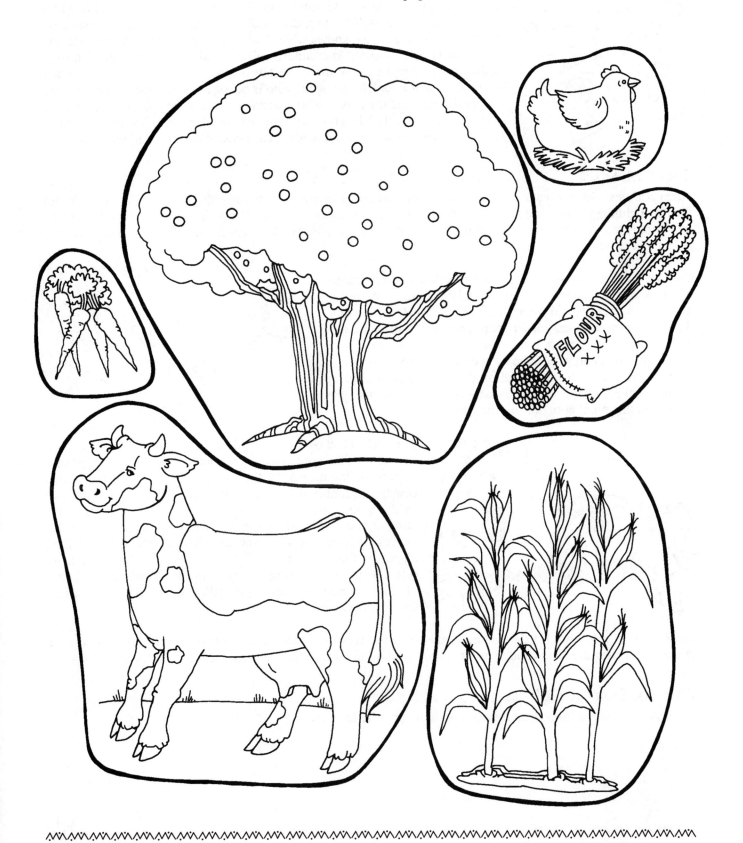

FLOUR
x x x

## Creative Movement

Make two copies and pass out the animal cards (patterns on page 37)—one to each child. If you have an odd number of children, either give three of one animal or participate yourself. The children look at the animal picture on their card and hide it so no one else knows what kind of animal they are. When you say "Barnyard Boogie Woogie," the children all pretend to be the animal on their cards. They may make the sound as well as act like the animal. As they are acting, they must also look for someone who is acting the same way. Without using any words, they find the person who is acting like the same animal. The partners separate from the rest of the group and watch while the others find their partners. After the game, talk about what made it easy and difficult to find their partners.

## Cognitive Skills

*Farm Riddles:* You (or a student) reflect on things on the farm and choose one thing. Give a hint about it and the other children may ask questions or guess what it is. For example, say, "I am thinking of something on the farm that is red" (or soft or loud or smelly, etc.). When someone in the class names the farm item, he or she may reflect and choose the next item.

*Counting Farm Animals:* This game practices numeral recognition skills. Copy page 37 with the nine farm animals. Write one numeral on each animal from 1 to 9. (Copy it twice if the children recognize numbers higher than nine.) Place the nine animals on the floor where everyone can see them. The object is for the children to identify the animals in order from one to nine and place them on a farm scene. Call on different children to place the next animal on the scene. For extra reinforcement, draw the corresponding number of dots on the card.

*Catch the Cow Game:* You will need a stuffed cow or other farm animal for this game. Divide the class in two even groups and have them line up side by side facing each other. Put the stuffed cow in the center of the two groups. Give each child a number so the groups are using the same numbers. When you call a number, the child with that number from each group races for the cow. Whoever gets the cow races back to line without getting tagged by the other person. If the cow makes it back, the team gets a point. If the person is tagged, the other team gets a point. After all the numbers have been called, count the points to find the winning team.

*Field Trip:* Visit a farm. Let the children experience the sounds, smells, and sights of the farm. Encourage the children to notice the colors and textures (gooey mud, rough wood, soft animals, etc.) around the farm.

## Dismissal from Circle Time

Dismiss the children from circle time by children's favorite farm animal.

cow

horse

duck

hen

sheep

goat

dog

cat

pig

# Feet and Movement

## Building Language Experience

*Talk About Feet:* There are 52 bones in your feet, so feet can move in many different ways. Our feet help us balance. Even when we are walking normally, we use our feet for balance. We can also walk on tip-toes or on our heels. What can we do with our feet? Ask the children to demonstrate different ways our feet can move: We can have loud feet, quiet feet, quick feet, slow feet, sneaky feet, wiggly feet, backwards feet, and so on. Our feet aren't as coordinated as monkey feet. How do other animals use their feet?

*Compare Feet and Shoes:* Have students take off their shoes and socks. Talk about what the feet look like. Some people have long feet, some have short feet, others have wide or narrow feet. Sort the class into two groups: kids whose second toe is longer than their big toe and those whose big toe is longer. Challenge students to find someone whose shoes are the same length.

## Literature

Read *The Foot Book* by Dr. Seuss. This book has a fun rhythm and silly pictures. After reading, count the feet in the circle right now. Have everyone find their right foot and their left foot. Have everyone move their left and right feet to the patterns in the book. They can also tap their toes to the rhythm in the book.

## Music and Movement

Play "Hokey-Pokey."
> You put your right foot in, you put your right foot out.
> You put your right foot in and shake it all about.
> You do the hokey-pokey and you turn yourself around.
> That's what it's all about.
>> *(In the next verse, you put your left foot in.)*

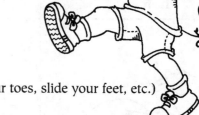

Sing "If You're Happy and You Know it."
> If you're happy and you know it, stomp your feet.
> If you're happy and you know it, stomp your feet.
> If you're happy and you know it, your feet will surely show it.
> If you're happy and you know it, stomp your feet.

*(Other verses:* Replace "stomp your feet" with tap your toes, wiggle your toes, slide your feet, etc.)

## Creative Movement

*A New Way to Walk:* Encourage children to move in different ways with their feet: hop, gallop, slide, skip, and walk with toes pointing out. Encourage them to be creative with their foot movements as you play music.

*Pattern Walking:* With everyone standing in a circle, walk around in a circle with a pattern. For example, step, step, slide, step, step, slide. Teach the students the pattern and then have everyone walk in the pattern together. Allow others to teach and lead a pattern around the circle.

## Cognitive Skills . . . . . . . . . . . . . . . . . . . . . . . . . . . . . . . . . . . . . . . . . . . .

**Shoe Sort:** Ask each student to take off one shoe and put it in the center of the circle for everyone to see. Talk about the different styles and colors of shoes. Ask the children to name different descriptions of the shoes while you write them on index cards. Sort shoes by the descriptions, allowing students to take turns putting shoes in the correct piles (for example, shoes with laces, shoes with Velcro, and slip-on shoes). Mix up the shoes and sort a new way.

**Counting:** Ask everyone to sit in the circle with his or her feet in front. Count the number of feet in the room. Ask the children with a certain color or style of shoes to hide their feet. Count the number of feet showing now. Repeat with a different group of feet hidden. More advanced: count the number of toes by counting by tens.

**Attribute Mystery:** Think of one attribute of the children's shoes, but don't tell them what you are thinking. Tap all the children wearing shoes with that attribute indicating that they are to stand in the center of the circle. Ask the other children to guess what all those shoes have in common. For example: all the shoes in the center have laces. Have those children go back to the circle. Repeat by thinking of a new attribute for them to guess.

**Sock Puppets:** Have each child bring in an old, clean sock. Teach children how to put their hand in and make a mouth. While the hands are in the socks, draw dot eyes with permanent markers. Have the puppets talk to each other and recite a familiar rhyme. Explore how to give the puppets personality. During play time, children may glue on felt clothes, hats, or yarn hair that you cut in advance.

**Cooperative Shoe Race:** Mix up all of the children's shoes in the center of the circle. Challenge the students to work together to find and put on their own shoes before the timer rings (set for three minutes). Children may help each other put them on and tie them, if necessary. If they get done in time, reward the children by letting them do their favorite activity. Play again and try to improve the time by working together more. Alternatively, have the children hide their eyes while you spread the shoes around the room. They must find their shoes and put them on before the time is up.

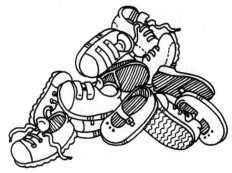

## Art . . . . . . . . . . . . . . . . . . . . . . . . . . . . . . . . . . . . . . . . . . . . . . . . . . . . . . . .

Paint footprints on paper. You will want some adult help with this if you are working with more than four or five children. Have the children take off their shoes and socks and roll up their pants. Set up a shallow pan of paint for children to step in. Set it next to the paper. On the other end of the paper, set up a dishtub with soapy water. Children step in the paint, walk on the paper, and step into the water. Dry their feet as they step out of the dishtub of soapy water. They may paint two feet next to each other. This makes a good animal face to which you add ears and facial features. Or have them take several steps as if walking. Once the prints are dry, they may be cut out and hung from a mobile.

# Flowers

## Building Language Experience

Pass around some soft and fragrant flower petals, such as rose petals. Let the children experience the feeling and smell and then talk about the color and shape of the petals. Talk about flowers. What color flowers have they seen? What kinds of flowers can they name and describe? It is helpful to have a poster of different flowers or a book with color photos of different flowers. Look at different shades of the same color. Do flowers come in all colors of the spectrum? Talk about (and bring in samples of) some flowers that are currently in bloom in your area. Compare the sizes, shapes, colors, and smells of different flowers.

Pass around magnifying glasses and flowers. Have several on hand so the children can spend some time looking for details. Point out the veins in the petals, the reproductive parts, the inside of the stem (if cut). Allow children to talk about what they see and ask questions. Count the number of petals and other parts.

## Senses

Compare the scent of two different flowers. Some flowers, such as hyacinths and lilies, are strong smelling. Have children compare these smells with the scent of a rose or violet.

## Literature

Read *The Reason for a Flower* by Ruth Heller. With rhyme and beautiful illustrations, young children learn many things about flowers.

## Nursery Rhymes

"Mary, Mary Quite Contrary, How does your garden grow?
With Silver bells and cockle shells and pretty maids all in a row."
As an extension, paint gardens with green stems and use sponges cut in bell and shell shapes for the flowers.

"Roses are red; violets are blue. Sugar is sweet and so are you."

## Creative Movement

Make a simple maypole to dance around in celebration of spring. You will need a two-meter piece of ribbon for each child (or you may have half the class dance at a time). Tie the ribbons together at one end and tape securely to the top of a stick (a broom stick works). You may also tape silk or plastic flowers to the top to make it more authentic. Hold the pole with the ribbons at the top. Each child holds the end of one ribbon and they skip and dance around the pole. They will have to move cooperatively to make it work. (Alternatively, tie the ribbons to a hula-hoop.)

*Flower Movement:* Have the children pretend to be flowers. Have them curl up as seeds and then sprout roots going down (wiggle their toes) and then uncurl as a stem goes up slowly in the warm sun. Then have them uncurl more and spread their arms to form leaves. Then as they grow a bud, which opens up to face the sun, they lift their heads. Then the flowers sway gently in the warm breeze. Then a bee comes by and gathers nectar and carries pollen to other flowers. (Move around the room and touch their heads.) Soon the flower dries up and drops its seeds on the ground. Those seeds will soon sprout and grow into new flowers.

## Science

During center time, cut the bottom of the stem of a white carnation. Put the stem in a clear vase of water. Add a few drops of food coloring. Ask the students to predict what will happen over time. Put the vase in a secure place where the children can observe it throughout the rest of the day and the next day. Talk about any changes you see. The stem of the flower contains veins that carry water from the roots up to the flower. You can see the capillary action when the colored water moves up the stem and into the petals.

## Cognitive Skills

*Planting Flowers:* Put a tub of dirt or florist's foam in the center of the circle. Have a number of plastic flowers nearby. Choose a number and have one student "plant" that many flowers in the tub. Count the planted flowers with the whole class. Then choose a different number and another student to "plant" that many flowers.

*Flower sort:* You will need a variety of plastic flowers for this activity. Display the flowers on the floor in the center of the circle. Have children propose different ways to sort the flowers (color, number of petals or leaves, size, type, etc.) and then sort them into vases or florist's foam. Challenge the students to find unique ways to sort the flowers.

## Games

*Play "Pin the Petal on the Flower."* Tape a 10" colored circle on the wall at about the height of the children's heads. Cut out petal shapes from construction paper. Put a piece of poster putty or tape on a petal. Have one blindfolded child at a time try to tape a petal near the center of the flower. Write student names on the petals and leave them up as the game continues.

*Where Is the Seed?* One person is the gardener and three others will be squirrels that hide their eyes while the gardener plants a sunflower seed. The other children sit in the circle with their hands cupped in front of them. While the three squirrels aren't looking, the gardener puts the seed in one child's hands. The three squirrels are called back and open hands to try to find the seed. The squirrel who finds the seed is the new gardener. The children in the circle may say the following chant to let the squirrels know they can come and look.

Chant:

Gardener, gardener, plant the seed.
Hide it where the squirrels can't see.
Squirrels may look where noses lead.
Find that seed near your tree.

## Center Activities

*Painting:* Paint a sunflower with a large yellow circle and little yellow petals all around. Add a green stem with leaves. Then, dot the yellow circle with black paint to make the seeds.

*Play dough:* Form a ball for the center of the flower and flatten it. Roll little balls and flatten them to form the petals around the center circle.

# Hands

## Building Language Experience

Talk about the differences and similarities between hands. Children will enjoy comparing hand size with others. Talk about the names of the different fingers and the jobs the fingers do. What is a pinky finger good for, anyway? Why are fingers different sizes? Our hands are able to move in many different ways and hold onto things. What can we do with our hands that most animals can't do?

Put a variety of mittens in the center of the circle. You can use real mittens or mitten shapes cut out of a variety of fabrics. (Pattern found on page 44.) Allow the children to take turns finding matching mittens. Put the mittens in a center for children to later explore on their own.

***Sensory Exploration***: Pass around gardening gloves, rubber gloves, leather gloves and mittens of different materials (wool, fleece, acrylic, etc.) for children to smell and feel. (Wool mittens have a smell that recalls childhood memories to me.) Talk about the different materials. What are the mittens and gloves used for? For what other purposes is this type material used? (sweaters, coats, sweatshirts) Why are they different colors?

***Finger Puppets***: Use the duck patterns on page 43. Cut five ducks out of yellow felt. Glue one duck to each finger of a glove. Show the stated number of ducks on the glove as you sing the "Five Little Ducks" song.

> Five little ducks went out to play
> Over the hills and far away.
> Mother duck called, "quack, quack, quack"
> And only four little ducks came back.
>
> Four little ducks went out to play . . .

Sing the song until there are no ducks. The final verse brings all the ducks back. Open the glove on the last line to show all five ducks.

> No little ducks went out to play
> Over the hills and far away.
> Mother duck called, "quack, quack, quack"
> And five little ducks came running back.

"Where Is Thumbkin?" (to the tune of "Are You Sleeping?")
> Where is Thumbkin? Where is Thumbkin?
> > *(make a fist with thumb up. Bend thumb in rhythm with the song.)*
> Here I am. Here I am.
> > *(The other thumb comes out of its fist and bends to the beat.)*
> How are you today, sir?  *(first thumb bends as if talking)*
> Very well, I thank you.  *(second thumb bends as if talking)*
> Run away, run away.  *(first thumb goes behind back, then second thumb)*

Sing other verses about the other fingers: Where is pointer? Where is ring finger? Where is pinky?

# Five Little Ducks

Directions found on page 42.

**Hands**

Read, recite, or act out the Mother Goose rhyme, "Three Little Kittens." Have children hold up, hide, and pretend to wash mittens as you read. Copy the mitten patterns below. Have each child color the mittens. Depending on children's ability, encourage them to color the two mittens the same and with a pattern.

## Cognitive Skills Games . . . . . . . . . . . . . . . . . . . . . . . . . . . . . . . . . . . . . . .

*Finger Counting:* Hold up a card with a numeral or a number of objects printed on it. The number should be between zero and ten. The students read the card and hold up the same number of fingers.

## Art . . . . . . . . . . . . . . . . . . . . . . . . . . . . . . . . . . . . . . . . . . . . . . . . . . . . . . . . .

Use the recipe below to make finger paint. Use finger paints to make hand prints.

Finger Paint: mix 1 cup clear, liquid dish detergent with 3 Tbsp. cornstarch. Pour the clear paint into separate cups and add food coloring to each.

## Food . . . . . . . . . . . . . . . . . . . . . . . . . . . . . . . . . . . . . . . . . . . . . . . . . . . . . . . . .

Frost and eat lady fingers. Make finger foods.

# Mitten Patterns
Directions found on page 42.

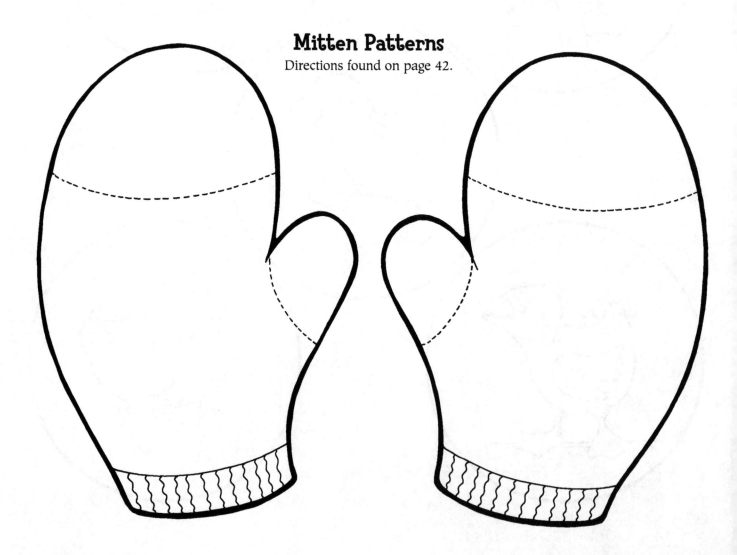

# Hats

## Building Language

**Experience:** Put on an unusual hat for circle time and encourage the children to talk about it. What does it look like? When would you wear this hat? Talk about different kinds of hats. Different jobs require hats. We wear hats for different kinds of weather. Some sports and hobbies require special hats. Ask who likes to wear hats. Talk about what kinds of hats they wear. Tell them that tomorrow they can wear their hats to school.

**Wear-a-Hat Day:** Sort the hats in different ways. Ask the children to look around at all the hats and have them name attributes, such as "has a brim." Write "brim" on an index card and have all the children put the hats with brims by the label. Have them name several attributes, one at a time, to sort different ways (flowered, sports, dress-up, sun, etc.).

Use the labels you wrote for the sorting activity as categories to make a floor graph. After all the hats are on the graph, discuss the data. Count the numbers and compare which categories have the most and least number of hats.

Pass around all the hats made of different materials. Compare the feeling of straw, felt, canvas, wool, and fleece, for example. Have the children describe the feeling (and smell) of different hats as they are passing them around.

## Literature

Read *A Three Hat Day* by Laura Geringer. Pay attention to the different kinds of hats in the story. How did hats make the characters feel? Does anything make you feel that way?

Read *Caps for Sale* by Esphyr Slobodkina. How much does a cap cost? Let the children try to balance more than one hat on their heads. Talk about the beginning and ending sounds of cap and hat.

## Music

Bring in a variety of different hats connected with occupations and sports, or duplicate page 46 showing the different types of hats (enlarge on the copier). As you hold up one hat, sing the following song with the children and fill in the type of person who wears that hat.

What Kind of Hat? (to the tune of "The Muffin Man.")

　　Oh, have you seen this kind of hat? This kind of hat? This kind of hat?

　　Oh, have you seen this kind of hat? It's worn _____ *(by a painter, at the beach, etc.).*

**Play Musical Hats:** Place a pile of hats in the center of the room. Pass a hat around the circle while the music plays. Stop the music. Whoever is holding the hat may pick a new hat from the center of the circle. Pass that hat while the music plays. As a variation, rather than play music, you can sing (to the tune of "Mulberry Bush"), "This is the way we pass the hat, pass the hat, pass the hat. This is the way we pass the hat so early in the morning."

# Hat Patterns
Directions found on page 45.

## Game

*Ball Toss:* Put a hat in the center of the circle. Use a small ball to throw in the hat. Let children take turns throwing the ball into the hat. Play music and cheer the children on.

*Cognitive Skills Game:* What Is Under the Hat? Hide an object under a hat and give the students a hint about what it is. They may ask questions and try to guess the object.

## Creative Movement

*Pass the Hat:* Duplicate the people wearing different hats on pages 47 and 48 so there is at least one hat-wearer per student. Cut out and fold, and put the squares in a hat. Turn on music while children pass the hat around the circle. Stop the music. Whoever is holding the hat takes out one paper and moves like the person wearing the hat in the picture. For example, the painter pretends to paint, and the cowboy pretends to ride a horse. Start the music and pass the hat again. Repeat until everyone has had a chance to pretend.

## Art

*Design a Hat:* You can pick up an inexpensive painter's hat from a paint store for each child. Or, make a cone-shaped hat from construction paper. Allow the children to decorate the hats with markers. For extra decorations, glue on feathers, plastic flowers, sequins, ribbons, and other recycled junk.

## Dismissal to the Next Activity

Dismiss children by naming types of hats they are wearing. For example, if you are wearing a baseball cap, you may go to the play dough center.

| astronaut | farmer | cow girl |

police officer

fire fighter

baseball player

painter

construction worker

gardener

# Insects

## Building Language Experience . . . . . . . . . . . . . . . . . .

Ask the children what they think of bugs. Some children are afraid of bugs, while others are fascinated. If possible, bring in an insect in a bug-viewing box. Pass it around and let the children describe what they see. Listen to stories about interesting bugs they have seen or experiences when they were stung or bitten by a bug.

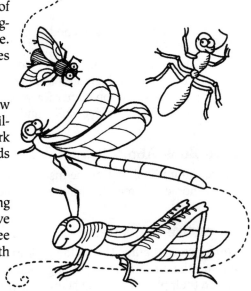

Talk about the good things that some bugs do for us. Most children know that bees make honey. Bees also play a very important role in the fertilization of many plants. The world would be in trouble without the work of the bees. Ladybugs are friends to gardeners when they eat the aphids that can destroy plants.

Look at colorful pictures of a variety of insects. Notice the interesting colors, shapes, and sizes. Talk about the body parts that all insects have in common: three body parts, wings, antennae, and six legs. The three body parts are head, thorax, and abdomen. Chant the body parts with the children as you tap your legs "head, thor-ax, and ab-do-men."

Discuss how to keep biting and stinging bugs away. When you play outside, it is helpful to wear bug repellent. If a bee or wasp is nearby, it is best not to try to swat at it. It is okay to move away but not to scare it.

## Literature . . . . . . . . . . . . . . . . . . . . . . . . . . . . . . . . .

Read *In the Tall, Tall Grass* by Denise Fleming. In this beautifully illustrated book, a caterpillar takes the reader on a tour of the tall grass and shows all the animals that live there. Although they are not all insects, the size perspective is interesting, and the sounds and rhymes make this a wonderful book for discussion.

Read *Ten Little Ladybugs* by Melanie Gerth. Little ones love the 3-D ladybugs that disappear one-by-one as you turn the pages. They also love the predictable rhymes and friendly animals that carry the ladybugs home.

## Creative Movement . . . . . . . . . . . . . . . . . . . . . . . . . . . .

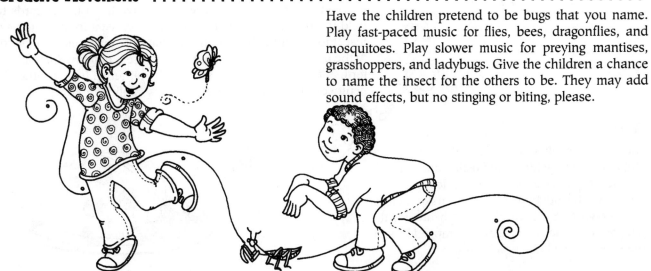

Have the children pretend to be bugs that you name. Play fast-paced music for flies, bees, dragonflies, and mosquitoes. Play slower music for preying mantises, grasshoppers, and ladybugs. Give the children a chance to name the insect for the others to be. They may add sound effects, but no stinging or biting, please.

## Finger Plays . . . . . . . . . . . . . . . . . . . . . . . . . . . . . . . . . . . . . . . . . . . . . . . . . . .

Shoo fly, don't bother me.
> *(touch your shoe, make a fly by putting the sides of your thumbs together and waving your open hands like wings, cross arms and look away)*

Shoo fly, don't bother me.          *(repeat motions—you have to be quick!)*
Shoo fly, don't bother me.          *(repeat motions)*
For I belong to somebody.          *(point to self and hug yourself)*

Ladybug, ladybug fly away home.
Your beautiful children are there all alone.
You're gathering dinner for your little tots
With bright orange shells and tiny black dots.

## Mini-Book About Insects . . . . . . . . . . . . . . . . . . . . . . . . . . . . . . . . . . . . . .

Make a mini-book out of the insects on page 51. Read the book several times with the children. Then they can take it home and read it with their families.

## Cognitive Skills Game . . . . . . . . . . . . . . . . . . . . . . . . . . . . . . . . . . . . . . . .

*Going on a Picnic:* The children sit in a circle. They take turns around the circle thinking of bugs and creepy-crawlies they will see on their picnic. They must think of critters that begin with the letters of the alphabet in order. "We're going on a picnic and I will see a(n) _____." For example, the first child says, "We're going on a picnic and I will see an ant." The second child may say, "We're going on a picnic and I will see a beetle." Continue around the circle until someone gets stuck on a letter. The other children may help or you may consult an insect guide. To make the game more challenging, the children must remember all the insects that came before them in order.

*Insect Patterns:* Duplicate the insects on page 52 and cut apart. Make at least four copies of the page. Glue the insects on large paper so they are easy to hold. Make insect patterns for the children to complete. Have four to six children stand up where everyone in the circle can see them. Give them insect cards to hold up in a simple pattern. Ask for volunteers to pick the next insect to continue the pattern. Repeat until everyone can identify the pattern. Repeat with a different insect pattern. Sample pattern: ant, beetle, butterfly, ant, beetle, butterfly. Increase the difficulty of the pattern as your students' ability improves.

## Food . . . . . . . . . . . . . . . . . . . . . . .

Ladybug Cupcakes: Bake cupcakes. Allow the children to frost with white frosting and sprinkle with red sugar. Use thin, rope licorice to make a line down the ladybug's back or to make six legs. Use brown M & Ms or black jellybeans for the dots on their backs. Place an unwrapped kiss on the edge for the ladybug's head.

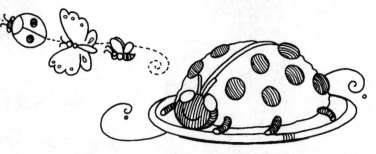

3

Yes, 1, 2, 3!

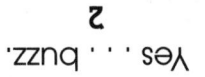

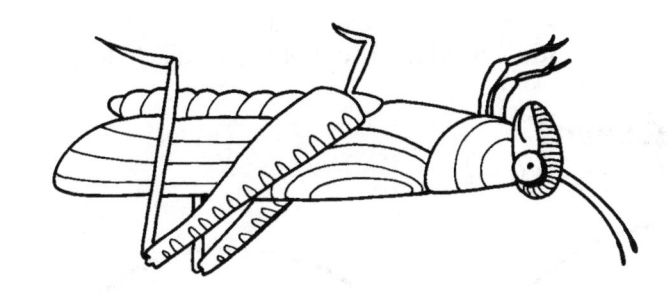

Do grasshoppers have three body parts?

Do dragonflies have large wings?

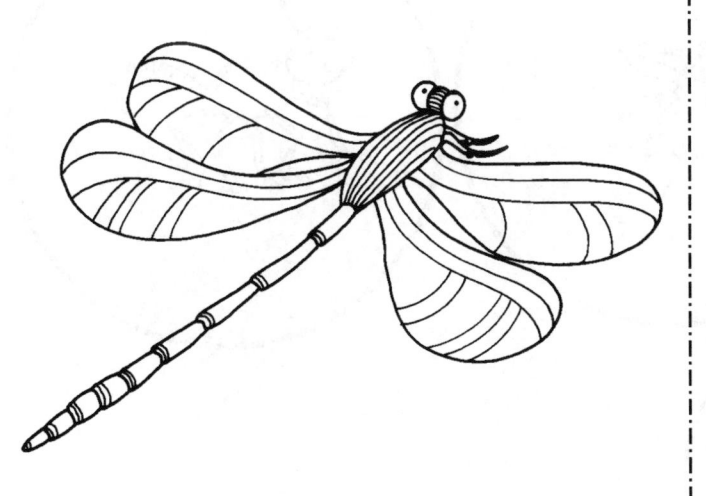

Yes, they do!
4

Do bees make a buzzing sound?

Yes . . . buzz.
2

Do ants work hard?

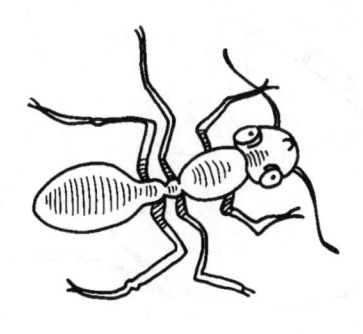

Yes, ants work hard!
1

## Art

***Fingerprint Insects:*** Use a stamp pad (or tempera paint on a paper towel) for children to make prints of their fingers and fine-tip markers to add insect details. Put three black fingerprints in a row for an ant. Add six legs, two eyes, and two antennae. For a ladybug, stamp one red print. Draw dots, lines on its back, six legs, and a tiny head with antennae. For a bee, stamp a yellow print. Draw black stripes and add wings and eyes. For butterflies, stamp two prints next to each other. Draw antennae between the "wings." For a dragonfly, stamp four prints in a cloverleaf shape. Draw a long, thin body between the two halves. Add a head made out of two small circles.

## Insect Patterns

Directions found on page 50.

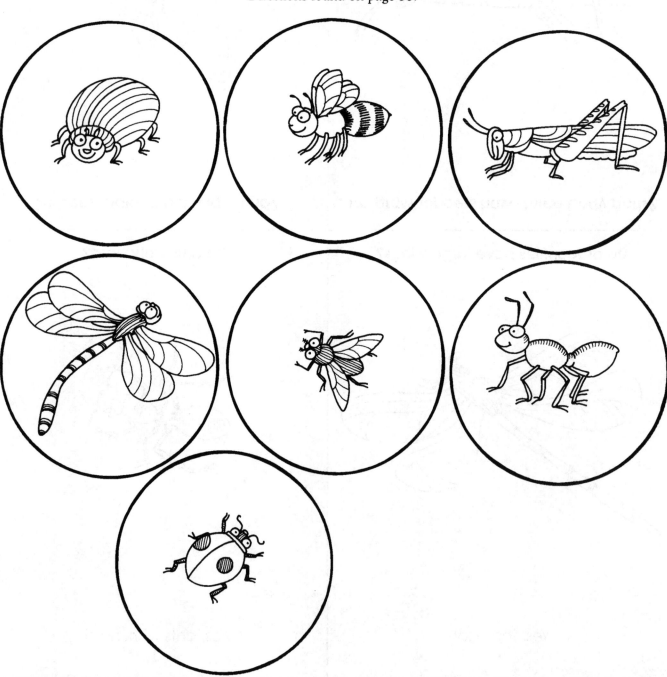

# Pond Life

## Building Language Experience . . . . . . . . . . . . . . . . . . . . . .

Talk about what animals live around a pond: ducks, beavers, frogs, salamanders, snakes, turtles, red-winged blackbirds, insects, spiders, butterflies, and so on. Look at pictures of the pond and describe the plants that grow there. Listen to children's stories about visiting the pond and catching tadpoles and frogs. Note: If turtles are removed from their homes, they should be returned to their exact home or they will not survive. Talk about the proper way to handle animals and plants that grow and live in the wild. Build in the children a respect for living things.

Talk about the sounds you might hear around a pond. Many children think that a frog says, "ribbit," but to get a sample of what different frogs really sound like go to the following Web site:

     http://www.naturesound.com/frogs/frogs.html

This site has photos of twelve different frogs and includes recordings of the sounds they make.

Show the children pictures or props to demonstrate how frogs and butterflies change through the cycles of their lives. Introduce the word "metamorphosis." Teach them to clap hands on their knees as they say the syllables of the word, "metamorphosis."

## Creative Movement . . . . . . . . . . . . . . . . . . . . . . . . . . . . .

Have the children curl up and act like eggs. The tiny egg hatches, and the children can crawl around and pretend to eat like caterpillars. Tell that after several weeks, the caterpillar spins a cocoon and stays inside for two weeks. When it comes out of the cocoon it is now a beautiful butterfly. At first their wings are wet and crumpled. After a couple hours the wings will straighten and dry out. The children can spread their wings and fly around like butterflies.

## Music and Rhyme . . . . . . . . . . . . . . . . . . . . . . . . . . . . . .

Read *Over in the Meadow*. There are many book versions of this classic rhyme/story. Ezra Jack Keats illustrates a beautiful book for very young children. Jane Cabrera has a fun illustrated version that focuses on the counting aspect of the rhyme. This traditional rhyme/story takes place in a meadow near a pond. Raffi also sings a version of the rhyme.

## Finger Play . . . . . . . . . . . . . . . . . . . . . . . . . . . . . . . . . .

Recite "The Itsy-bitsy Spider" and do the finger plays.

*Rowing Song:* Pair students up to row together. They sit down, face each other, put the soles of their feet together, and hold hands. One person leans back as the other leans forward while they sing "Row, row, row your boat." To make the song more appropriate, change the lyrics slightly to "Row, row, row your boat, gently round the pond. Careful while you row the boat; of frogs I'm very fond."

## Field Trip . . . . . . . . . . . . . . . . . . . . . . . . . . . . . . . . . . .

*Visit a pond in your area:* Observe the life and sounds of the pond. Look at the woods surrounding the pond as well. Observe the plants and animals. Discuss how the animals and plants change with the seasons.

## Cognitive Skills

Pond-life Riddles: Tell the children you are thinking of a plant or animal that lives or grows at the pond. Tell them one attribute of the plant or animal and allow them to guess and question you about the plant or animal. Allow other children to pick the pond life for others to guess.

*Butterfly Matching:* Use the butterfly pattern on page 55 to cut butterfly shapes. Use wallpaper sample books, construction paper, paper that you have texture painted, sandpaper, and other papers. Cut two butterflies out of each color/pattern. Allow students to take turns matching the butterflies.

## Games

*Play "Duck, Duck, Goose" Around the Circle.* One child touches the heads as he or she walks around the outside of the circle. At each touch, the person who is "it" says either duck or goose. If he or she says "goose," the goose jumps up and chases "it" around the circle. If the goose catches the person, the person who was "it" sits in the middle of the circle until someone else is tagged. If the person makes it around to sit in the goose's spot, the goose becomes "it." Variations: tadpole, tadpole, frog or caterpillar, caterpillar, butterfly. The children may hop or fly instead of run when picked from the circle.

*Hiding Around the Pond:* Designate the corners of the room as the pond, the forest, the meadow, and the air. One child is "it." Cover that child's eyes. "It" counts to ten while the other children scatter to the different designated areas. After saying "ten," the person whom is "it" names one of the places (still without looking). All the children who hid in that area must sit in the middle of the room. "It" begins counting again as the rest of the children scatter again to the pond, forest, meadow, or air. The game continues until only one child is left. That child becomes "it."

*Butterfly Metamorphosis:* Fold a paper and unfold so it has four squares. Have the children draw a leaf in the first box and glue a small, dried bean to represent the egg. In the second box, the children draw grass and plants that a caterpillar might eat. Also glue a spiral pasta on that square. In the third box, they draw a branch and glue a tube pasta hanging from the branch to represent a cocoon. In the fourth box, they draw a flower and glue a bow-tie pasta on the flower to represent a butterfly (laying its egg to start the cycle again).

## Painting

Students paint a blue pond of any shape. Use green paint to draw the grasses and cattails around the pond. After the paint dries, the students add details with markers: tops of cattails, animals, birds, insects, frogs, etc.

## Food

Make chocolate spiders. Melt 12 ounces of chocolate chips in a double boiler or the microwave. Remove from heat and gently stir in one can (3 oz.) of Chinese noodles. You may not be able to add the whole can of noodles. Drop from a spoon onto wax paper. Allow to cool before eating.

# Butterfly Pattern

Directions found on page 54.

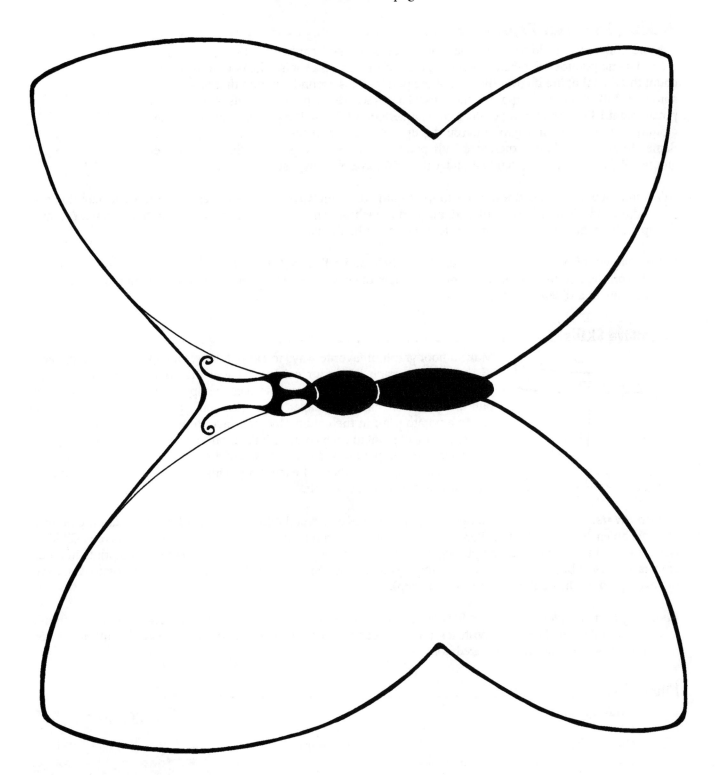

# Potatoes

## Building Language Experience

Ask the children this riddle: What has lots of eyes but still can't see? It's a potato. Pass around some potatoes of different sizes, colors, and types. Ask the students to look for and count the eyes that are all over the skin of the potato. Pass around a potato that has already sprouted. Talk about the purpose of the eyes. (That is where the potato sprouts to grow a new potato plant.) Talk about how potatoes grow underground. There is a green, leafy bush above ground and potatoes underground. You dig up potatoes when they are big enough to eat. Some children may have experience with potatoes and other vegetables that grow underground. Potatoes that are green just under the skin have been exposed to the sun.

Talk about how we eat potatoes. Brainstorm as many different ways to eat potatoes as the students can think of: mashed, baked, French fries, scalloped, au gratin, hash browns, etc. Why don't we eat potatoes raw? You may cut up a raw potato and let students taste it and describe the flavor.

Put the variety of potatoes in the center of the circle and talk about the differences. Allow students to propose ways to sort the potatoes (size, color, shape, number of eyes, type, etc.). Sort them into different groups and then sort them again a different way.

## Cognitive Skills

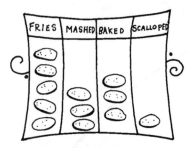

Make a floor graph of favorite ways to eat potatoes. Draw lines on a large piece of paper for a graph with four columns. Label the columns mashed, baked, French fries, and another way your class likes their potatoes. Cut two potatoes in half and put each half on a paper plate with some paint. Allow each child to stamp a potato print in the column by their favorite way to eat potatoes. Use a different color of paint in each column. Talk about the data on the finished graph. What way to eat potatoes do the most children prefer? Which is the least favorite? How many are there of each kind? This is a symbolic graph, which is more abstract than a floor graph.

*Potato Prints:* Stamp a different number of potato prints on several different sheets of paper. Count the number of prints on each page with the children. Write the number on the page. Later, put the pages in a center. Children can count and match numbers by putting objects on each potato print. For variety, make potato prints in different shapes. Use a butter knife to sketch a simple shape about one cm deep into the cut side of a potato. Cut away the extra potato outside the sketch (one cm deep).

*Counting French Fries:* Cut French fries out of cardboard or a yellow sponge. Obtain French fry holders from a local restaurant (or make some). Write a number on each holder. Allow the children to take turns putting the correct number of fries into the numbered holders.

## Finger Play

### Underground

Carrots, turnips, onions, too       *(crying with fists wiping eyes)*
Grow as beets and potatoes do.       *(fist over fist)*
Leaves growing up, roots shooting down.
     *(hands come together and separate as they move up, opposite for roots)*
Dig up veggies from the ground.      *(digging motion)*

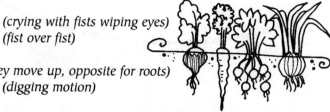

## Literature

Read *Growing Vegetable Soup* by Lois Ehlert. There are lots of things to count and name in this simple book. After reading, you may enjoy making vegetable soup as a class. Ask students to each bring in a baggie filled with a cut-up vegetable. Cook in chicken broth and add noodles or rice.

## Science

Cut up potatoes into pieces. Give each student a piece with an eye on it. Each student puts the potato chunk in a resealable plastic bag with a wet paper towel. Write names on the bags and put them in the sun for several days. Watch for sprouts. Keep track of the number of days until a sprout is first observed. Count the number of new sprouts each day.

## Games

*Hot Potato:* While you play music, the children pass a potato around the circle. They pretend it is very hot (just out of the oven) and pass it quickly, so they don't burn their fingers. When the music stops, the person holding the potato may name a different adjective (soft, prickly, cold, slimy, sticky, or hot). When the music starts again, the children pass the potato as if it felt like that adjective.

*Mashed Potatoes:* This game is fun and silly but is also great for exercise and listening skills. Name different ways to eat potatoes while the children hop around the circle area. When you name mashed potatoes, they have to fall to the floor and wiggle around. As a variation, name vegetables or favorite foods while they hop. (A child may take your place naming things.) Another variation: when you name "mashed potatoes," if there are any children who don't fall to the ground on cue, they have to sit out until the next round.

*Potato Drop:* Set your class up into two to four groups. Give each group a large potato and line them up across the room from a bucket or tub. On a cue, the first person from each team must carry their potato between their legs across the room and drop it in their bucket. If they use hands or drop the potato, they must go back to the starting line. After the potato is in the bucket, they pick it up and bring it to the next person in line. The team that is done first is the winner.

## Sensory Tub

Put potatoes and dirt in a sensory tub. Provide spoons, small shovels, tongs, and other tools for digging up and planting potatoes. Make sure you have newspapers around to catch the mess.

# Pumpkins

## Building Language Experience . . . . . . . . . . . . . . . . . . . . . . . . . . . .

Ask the children to tell about their experiences with pumpkins. Have they ever carved a pumpkin, eaten pumpkin pie, or grown a pumpkin in their garden? Pass a small pumpkin around the circle. Pass a large pumpkin around the circle. Talk about the differences in size and color and heaviness. Ask the children to tell you how they know that one pumpkin is heavier than the other. Lead them to suggest that you weigh the pumpkins on a scale. Talk about what kind of scale would work best for the job. Weigh the pumpkins and talk about which number is bigger.

Use a piece of yarn to measure the horizontal circumference of the smaller pumpkin. Ask the children whether it will take more or less yarn to wrap around the larger pumpkin. Try it out. Compare the lengths of the two yarns used. Use yarn to measure around the pumpkins vertically. Compare those lengths.

Set the pumpkins on top of several layers of newspaper. Cut the top off the pumpkins and allow the children to smell the pumpkins. Allow the children to take turns scooping out the insides and separating the seeds. Save the seeds from each pumpkin in a separate container. Compare the seeds to determine which pumpkin had more seeds.

## Finger Play . . . . . . . . . . . . . . . . . . . . . . . . . . . . . . . . . . . . . . . . .

Five little pumpkins sitting on a gate.
 *(Hold up five fingers.)*
The first one said, "oh my it's getting late."
 *(Hold up one finger, then point to a watch.)*
The second one said, "there are witches in the air."
 *(Hold up two fingers, then point to a witch flying across the sky.)*
The third one said, "but I don't care."
 *(Hold up three fingers and then shrug.)*
The fourth one said, "Let's run and run and run."
 *(Hold up four fingers and make running movements with your arms.)*
The fifth one said, "I'm ready for some fun."
 *(Hold up five fingers and circle index finger in the air.)*
Then ooooh went the wind and out went the light.
 *(cup hands around mouth for wind and clap hands for lights out)*
Five little pumpkins rolled out of sight.
 *(roll hands around each other)*

## Literature . . . . . . . . . . . . . . . . . . . . . . . . . . . . . . . . . . . . . . . . . .

Read *The Berenstain Bears and the Prize Pumpkin* by Stan and Jan Berenstain.

## Field Trip . . . . . . . . . . . . . . . . . . . . . . . . . . . . . . . . . . . . . . . . . . .

Visit a pumpkin patch. Observe how pumpkins grow on vines and rest on the ground when they are too heavy for the plant. Talk about how they grow green and ripen into orange. Notice the different sizes. Ask the grower to explain how they care for pumpkins and what makes some grow larger.

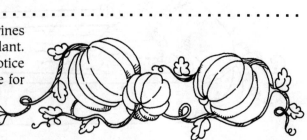

## Creative Movement

*Pumpkins:* Have students roll up to look like a small pumpkin. They should gradually get bigger, but try to keep a round shape. The pumpkins turn orange in October. Then when the pumpkins are big, have them roll away from their vine with a somersault (or rolling on their sides).

## Cognitive Skills

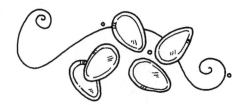

Put small handfuls of dried or roasted pumpkin seeds in cups. Give a cup to each child along with a pumpkin shape drawn on an orange sheet of paper. Ask the children to count their seeds. Tell them how many seeds to place on the pumpkin shape. Practice simple addition and subtraction as you tell them to add or take away seeds and count their totals each time.

## Game

You will need a small round pumpkin for this passing game. Have the children stand in a circle facing the back of the person next to them. They pass the pumpkin around the circle by passing it under their legs to the person behind them. You can start two pumpkins on opposite sides of the circle for a faster-pace game.

*Pumpkin Bags:* While in circle time, give each child a paper lunch bag. Teach them how to wrinkle up newspaper and stuff it in the bag. They should stuff it so it is round, but they can still twist the top closed. Tie the bags closed with green yarn or twist ties. At the table, give the children orange tempera paint and large brushes to paint the bags orange beneath the tie. Give them green or brown paint for above the tie (for the stem). When the paint is dry, they can color black features with a marker or glue on black paper shapes for the features.

## Painting

Decorate small, real pumpkins with paints. Paint pens work well but are expensive. Tempera paints also work well.

# Shapes

## Building Language Experience . . . . . . . . . . . . . . . . . . . . . . . . . . . . . . . . . . . . . .

Talk about shapes with which the children are familiar: square, circle, oval, triangle, rectangle, octagon, trapezoid, and any others you have taught. Review with the children the number of sides and corners of each. Talk about the difference between an oval and a circle and a rectangle and a square. Draw one shape on a piece of sandpaper. Pass the sandpaper around for the children to trace with their index finger. Repeat with other shapes.

Get some inexpensive sunglasses and punch out the lenses. Give a couple students the "shape detective glasses" and a pointer stick. Challenge them to find shapes around the room. When they find a shape (rectangle book cover, circle on the clock, etc.), they point to it and tell the class what shape it is. If detectives are having trouble finding shapes, they can get hints from the kids sitting in the circle. Take turns being shape detectives.

## Cooperative Challenge . . . . . . . . . . . . . . . . . . . . . . . . . . . . . . . . . . . . . . . . . . .

Challenge students to form different giant shapes with a large loop of elastic. You can buy elastic at the fabric store (half-inch width works well) by the yard. Cut a piece about five feet (two meters) long. Bring the ends together so the elastic forms a loop. Attach the ends with a safety pin. Choose four students to work together to form a square with the elastic. Choose three students to form a triangle with the elastic. Repeat with other shapes and different numbers of students. The other students can give hints to make the shapes more perfect. The shapes may be horizontal or vertical. Try a circle with a large number of children. Once they understand how to do it, sit back and let the children work it out.

## Cognitive Skills . . . . . . . . . . . . . . . . . . . . . . . . . . . . . . . . . . . . . . . . . . . . . . . . .

Cut large and small shapes out of construction paper, wallpaper samples, or other interesting paper. Cut a few different triangles so children realize that sometimes the sides are the same length, and sometimes none of the sides are the same length. Cut a rectangle that is wide and another that is tall. Talk about one shape at a time. Count the corners and sides.

*Watch Carefully:* Use the cut-out shapes to play an observation game. Put several shapes on a tray for the students to look at. Secretly remove one shape. Ask the children to figure out which shape you removed.

## Art . . . . . . . . . . . . . . . . . . . . . . . . . . . . . . . . . . . . . . . . . . . . . . . . . . . . . . . . . .

Provide different size circles for the children to trace on paper. They should overlap the circles. Show the children how to color each space a different color. With crayons, they can color different textures, too. Zig-zags, dots, and swirls create the impression of different textures. For more variety, they may glue small objects, sand, or glitter in some of the spaces. Try this activity with other shapes. It looks best if there is only one shape repeated on one paper.

## Game . . . . . . . . . . . . . . . . . . . . . . . . . . . . . . . . . . . . . . . . . . . . . . . . . . . . . . . . . .

*Shape Concentration:* Duplicate two copies of page 61. Cut out shape cards. Lay them facedown and ask children to pick up two cards. If they are identical shapes, the child may keep the cards. If not, turn the cards facedown again and the next child has a turn.

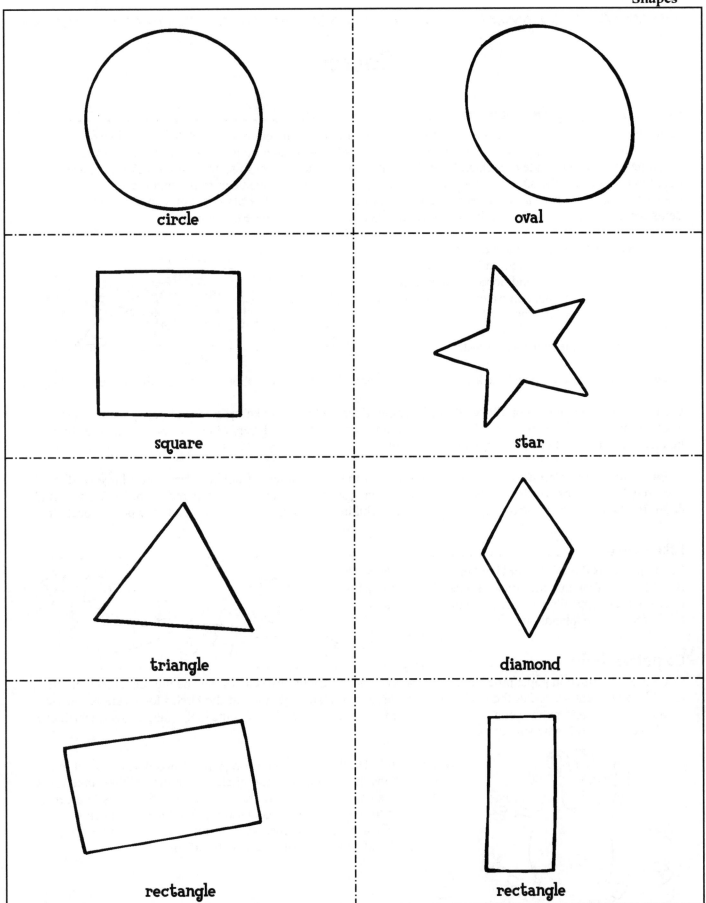

circle

oval

square

star

triangle

diamond

rectangle

rectangle

CD-0206 *It's Circle Time!*

# Space

## Building Language Experience . . . . . . . . . . . . . . . . . . . . . . . . . . . . . . . . . . . . . . . . . . . . . . . . . . . . . . . .

Show the students a model or picture of the solar system. Point out the earth and explain that we live on a planet among other planets. Our planet is the only planet that has life and water on it. It is often called the water planet. The other planets are made of rock and gas. The only way we have to get to space is on a rocket or space shuttle. Show pictures of the space shuttles and rockets. Explain that we have been to the moon and flown around the earth, but no person has ever been to another planet. Name the other planets. You can share with the students what you know about the other planets. Here is a rhyme to introduce the planets:

> Nine planets spin 'round a star.
> Mercury is close; Pluto and Neptune are far.
> The Earth is blue and home to me and you.
> Venus is burning; Saturn with rings is turning.
> Jupiter is big and cocky; Mars is red and rocky.
> Uranus is cold and looks green.
> These are the planets scientists have seen.

Allow the children some time to ask questions and share what they know about space and the planets.

We know that no one lives on those other planets, but people like to make up stories about space creatures, or aliens, that live far away in other galaxies. We can imagine that they look very different from us. Let the children be creative and talk about what they might look like.

***Taking Turns and Counting:*** Cut circles to represent the nine planets of different sizes on a large cardboard box. Play beanbag toss by tipping the box up and allowing students to toss a beanbag into the holes. They should count up the number of points they earn. Encourage children to cheer each other on and tally points together.

## Literature . . . . . . . . . . . . . . . . . . . . . . . . . . . . . . . . . . . . . . . . . . . . . . . . . . . . . . . . . . . . . . . . . . . . . . . . . . .

Read *The Sky Is Full of Stars* or *What the Moon Is Like* or *The Big Dipper* by Franklyn Mansfield Branley. These nonfiction books that are appealing to young children (four and up) are full of facts and explanations.

## Cognitive Skills . . . . . . . . . . . . . . . . . . . . . . . . . . . . . . . . . . . . . . . . . . . . . . . . . . . . . . . . . . . . . . . . . . . . . .

Cut out of construction paper nine circles of various sizes and colors. Two circles may be the same color, but they should be different sizes. Put the circles on a tray and let the students look at the circles for a couple minutes. Cover the circles and remove one secretly. Uncover the circles and let the students look again to guess which one you have removed (name size and color).

***Alien Match:*** Duplicate the aliens on page 64 two times and cut apart. Put the aliens in the center of the circle. Have the children take turns matching the pairs of aliens that are identical. Put the cards in a center for children to play a memory game during free time. Focus on some of the aliens for a counting activity. Count together the number of eyes, antennae, heads, toes, etc. on the different aliens.

## Games

**Parachute Fun:** Assign each child the name of a planet so two students have the same planet. Have the students stand in any order around a parachute. Name a planet. The children lift the parachute and the two who have that planet switch places in the circle. Name another planet and repeat until all the planets have switched. If you don't have a parachute, just have the children switch places in the circle (or they may orbit the circle before they sit down in the other planet's spot).

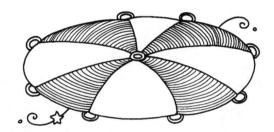

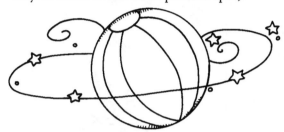

**Planet Ball:** Split the class in two teams that form lines. Assign each child a planet so players on opposite teams have the same planet. You stand in the middle of the two teams and throw a ball (the sun) up in the air and call out a planet name. The children with that planet name race to catch the ball. The child who catches the ball wins a point for his or her team.

## Creative Movement

Let the children pretend to be rockets taking off for space. They squat down while everyone counts down from ten to one. They gradually rise up and say "blast off!" while they jump in the air.

You can make this an outdoor game. Draw two lines. Have all the children stand behind one line facing the other. Choose one child to be the mission control commander. The commander stands behind the opposite line and tells the rockets to get into their launch positions. The children squat and count down as described. When they blast off, they run to the opposite line. Whoever gets there first is the next commander.

**Make a Space Bottle:** Clean out a small, plastic soda pop bottle. Fill the bottle about 3/4 full with light corn syrup. Add tiny stars and planets confetti (available at stationery stores), plastic rockets, or planets. Fill the bottle to the top with water. Add blue food coloring, if desired. Put the cap on and tip the bottle back and forth to watch things move as if in space.

## Painting

Let the children paint the planets. They can paint nine circles in different colors (red, blue, green). They can paint some with rings around them.

## Dismissal

Dismiss students by naming planets and other space terms. Students whose name begins with the same sound as _____, may go to centers.

# Aliens
Directions found on page 62.

# Teddy Bears

## Building Language Experience ....................................

Bring in a teddy bear (preferably one that was yours when you were a child) to share with the children. Ask them to tell you what a teddy bear is for. Talk about the color and texture of the teddy bear. Are all teddy bears the same as this one? Listen to children describe to each other how their teddy bears differ. Invite them to bring in their own favorite teddy bears the next time you meet.

When children bring in their own bears, encourage them to ask and answer questions about each other's bears. Talk about colors and textures of the different bears. Ask the children to name attributes of the bears. Write the attributes on index cards (one description per card). Pick two cards and set them in the center of the circle for sorting. The students will take turns placing their bears by one of the cards. Discuss together what to do when a bear can be sorted into either category.

Talk about naming a teddy bear. How is the name chosen? Compare the names of the teddy bears the children brought in. What types of names are there? (people names, colors, made-up words, pet names, favorite characters, etc.) Try to sort bears by the types of names they have.

Use comparative language to describe the different teddy bears. Hold up one of the large teddy bears and say, "This bear is large." Ask the children to help you pick out a bear that is smaller than that bear and one that is larger than that bear. Repeat with other attributes such as straight, curly, curlier; smooth, fluffy, fluffier; light, dark, darker; and so on.

## Science ..............................................

*Mass:* Use a classroom balance scale to weigh some of the teddy bears. Count the number of masses it takes to balance a bear. Estimate the mass of a second bear based on the mass of the first.

*Linear:* Ask each child to estimate the height of his or her teddy bear by telling you how long to cut a piece of yarn. As you cut the yarn for them, the children take the yarn back to their bears and compare the length of the yarn to the length of the bear. Talk about whether the yarn was too long or too short. Allow them time to explore different measurements on their bears with the yarn. Can they wrap the yarn around the bear's head or tummy? Which is longer: the distance around the tummy or the head? Are its arms or legs longer? Let them explore and talk about what they discover.

## Music

Sing "Teddy Bear, Teddy Bear." While children sing, they can have their teddy bears act out the directions in the song. Or, have the children do the actions. See page 67 for teddy bear pattern.

> Teddy bear, teddy bear,
> Turn around.
> Teddy bear, teddy bear,
> Touch the ground.
> Teddy bear, teddy bear,
> Turn out the light.
> Teddy bear, teddy bear,
> Say goodnight.

## Creative Dramatics

Read two versions of *The Three Bears*. Compare the pictures and the stories. Talk about how they are different and the same. Divide the children into groups of four. Make sure there are three teddy bears in each group. Ask each group to pretend they are the three bears and Goldilocks. This is just creative play, not a presentation. Allow them enough time to act out the story. Some children may wish to continue their play into free time.

## Creative Movement

Pretend to be bears. Show children how to stand on their feet with their hands on the ground. Tell the children that bears "amble." When they walk, they move their right front leg and right back leg at the same time. This takes some coordination for the children. Turn on some slow music with a steady beat and let the children amble like bears. They can growl and scratch and sleep like bears, as well.

## Food

Make porridge for the students to taste. Use big, middle, and little voices to describe how hot the porridge is as you eat. "This porridge is too hot."

## Literature

Read *We're Going on a Bear Hunt* by Michael Rosen. There are many different versions available. Act out the story after you read it. Set up the classroom with the different obstacles for children to move through: a grassy area (wade through backpacks), a muddy area (a rug), a forest (chairs for trees), a snowstorm (hang streamers from the ceiling), a cave (under a table).

## Game

Have a teddy bear parade or picnic. Let the children find appropriate noisemakers, streamers, and batons for the parade. Use your housekeeping tablecloth and dishes for the picnic. Read *Teddy Bear's Picnic* by Mark Burgess. The appealing thing about this version of the classic is that on each page the children lift a flap to reveal a familiar song to sing at their picnic.

## Dismissal to the Next Activity

Dismiss children by naming attributes of their bears. For example, if your bear is wearing a shirt, you may go to the play dough table.

# Teddy Bear Pattern
Directions found on page 66.

# Transportation

## Building Language Experience

Ask the students to think of things that have wheels. Write down all the things they name on index cards. Sort the cards into meaningful categories: wheels under our feet, wheels without motors, four wheels. Talk about the fact that wheels help us move faster. Think of other ways we get around without wheels (or the wheels are just for landing and take off). Pose different questions about the best method to get to someone's house. For example, what is the best way to get to your grandma's house? For some children it may be by car, while for others it may be by plane or by foot. Discuss the reasons for the different answers.

Ask students to think about the ways we get around in terms of how fast they are. Duplicate page 70. Cut apart the cards. Put the cards in order from slowest to fastest (from roller skates to jet). There isn't one correct way to order, so involve the kids in discussion about which ways are faster.

Invite students to bring in one favorite toy car, truck, plane, or boat the next time you meet. Allow students to talk about their toys and ask questions of the other children. Sort the vehicles into categories. Sort again a different way.

## Creative Movement

Pretend to be airplanes. Have the students put out their arms and move around like airplanes. Encourage them to make airplane sounds as they move.

## Music and Movement

Have children sit down on the floor facing a partner. The partners hold hands and put their feet together. While they sing "Michael Row Your Boat Ashore," they lean forward and back in a cooperative rowing motion.

## Music

Sing "The Wheels on the Bus."

## Literature

Read *The Seals on the Bus* by Lenny Hort. This book provides a delightful twist on the song "The Wheels on the Bus." The illustrations are fun and children will want to sing along as you read/sing the book. It has a funny ending when skunks get on the bus.

## Cognitive Skills

Parking Garage: Decorate an old shoe box to look like a garage. Cut doors in the side for cars to drive in. Put a number card on the garage. Allow the children to take turns driving the correct number of toy cars into the garage. Change the number card so students can practice counting to different numbers.

## Mystery Sort

Think of a category for sorting vehicles, but don't tell the class. Put all the vehicles that fit your category in the center of the circle. Ask the children to guess what your sorting rule is. For example: blue vehicles, no wheels, or construction vehicles.

## Game

Pass the car: Choose one child to sit in the center of the circle with his or her eyes closed. The center child says, "green light," and the other children pass a car around the circle behind their backs. When the person in the center says "red light," the person with the car holds it. All the children should keep their hands behind their backs. The center person may open his or her eyes and try to guess who is holding the car. The person who is holding the car goes in the center next.

## Art

*Textured Wheels:* Use toy cars and trucks to make tracks on a piece of paper. Put paint on a paper plate, run a toy car's wheels through the paint and then drive the car over the paper to make tracks. Have a few different colors and cars so the students can put different tracks on their papers.

*Transportation Mural:* Tape a large sheet of butcher paper on the wall. Set up newspaper beneath it. Tell the class that you are going to make a scene together. In the scene there will be all kinds of transportation. First you need to paint in the backgrounds. "If we are going to have boats, what do we need? (water) If we have cars and trains, what do we need? (road and tracks) We will also need sky for the airplanes and balloons." Assign jobs to students of painting in the sky, land, train tracks, and water. They may wish to add trees, birds, and other things to the picture. Then, as they find pictures in magazines, they may glue on cutouts of a variety of vehicles. They may also draw and cut out pictures of boats, planes. Over the next few days, the mural will fill in with modes of transportation. Duplicate page 70 for children to color and cut out and add to the mural.

## Science and Literature

Read *Who Sank the Boat* by Pamela Allen. Put a tub of water in the center of the circle and float a boat in the water. Ask the children how many pennies they think the boat will hold before it tips over or sinks? Count the pennies as you put them in the boat until it sinks. (Check out your boat in advance to see how many pennies it will hold. If your boat is too seaworthy, it will take too many pennies to sink it. As an alternative, form a boat out of aluminum foil for this activity.) As an alternative to pennies, use plastic animals that you have in your classroom.

## Food

Make sailboat snacks with hard-boiled eggs, toothpicks, and American cheese. Cut the egg in half lengthwise. Use half of the egg for the boat hull. Cut the American cheese in half diagonally. Weave the toothpick through the cheese to make a mast and sail and stick the opposite end of the toothpick in the egg.

## Sensory Table

Put sand and construction vehicles in the sensory table/tub.

## Dismissal to the Next Activity

Dismiss children by naming the different ways they got to school. For example, children who walked to school may paint on the mural.

bike

motorcycle

boat

bus

car

truck

helicopter

airplane

balloon

# Trees

## Building Language Experience ..........................................................

Talk about the importance of trees. We use trees for shade and beauty as well as food. Animals use trees for homes and food. Trees (and plants) also provide us with air to breathe. Have the children help you think of things that grow on trees: apples, pears, oranges, lemons, walnuts, avocados, bananas, etc.

Talk about the reasons that trees are sometimes cut down. Tree roots can do a lot of damage to houses or sidewalks. Branches can get in the way of power lines or create too much shade in a yard. Once a tree is cut down, it also has many uses: firewood, lumber for building, wood for toys, tools, paper, and boxes. Some people cut down trees in the forest for a specific use. When they do that, they must cut only some of the trees and plant new ones to replace what they cut. If all the trees in a forest are cut down, the forest will be gone along with many animal homes. It takes many years for a tree to grow.

Ask children to close their eyes and picture a tree they know. It can be in their yard or neighborhood, in the woods, or their Christmas tree. What do they like about that tree? What does the tree look like, feel like, smell like, sound like? What kind is it and what is it used for? If possible, go outside and look at trees. Let the children hug a tree, feel its bark, and study what it looks like. Count the number of leaves on a branch or the number of branches on a small tree. Older children can measure the width of trees. Study the tree carefully so children can go inside and paint a picture of their tree.

## Letter Formation ..........................................................

Collect a variety of skinny, small twigs—straight and curved—in different lengths (under 30 cm). Name a letter of the alphabet and ask the students to take turns and use the twigs to form the letter on the floor in the center of the circle. It is helpful to have (large) samples of the letters in sight.

## Music and Movement ..........................................................

| | |
|---|---|
| I'm a little ash tree, tall and straight. | *(stand straight with arms at sides)* |
| These are my branches; these are my leaves. | *(put arms out one by one, then wiggle fingers)* |
| When my roots touch water, up they sip. | *(point toes on each foot)* |
| Sun and water help me grow. | *(make a sun overhead and stand on tiptoes)* |

## Literature ..........................................................

There are lots of realistic books to read about trees, but here are a couple imaginative stories that involve trees. Read *The Money Tree* by Sarah Stewart (illustrated by David Small). This is a wonderful story that follows the growth of a money tree from January to December. The tree grows in the yard of a woman who is guided by love of everything natural. If money did grow on trees, Miss McGillicuddy wouldn't change her habits.

Read *The Missing Mitten Mystery* by Steven Kellogg. Even though trees aren't the central part of this story, there is a wonderful section of the story in which the main character plants a mitten and grows a mitten tree. The character imagines what she would do with all the mittens.

∧∧∧∧∧∧∧∧∧∧∧∧∧∧∧∧∧∧∧∧∧∧∧∧∧∧∧∧∧∧∧∧∧∧∧∧∧∧∧∧∧∧∧∧∧∧∧∧∧∧∧∧

## Cognitive Skills Game . . . . . . . . . . . . . . . . . . . . . . . . . . . . . . . . . .

*Apple Tree Counting and Matching:* Make several copies of the treetop using the pattern below. Cut out from brown construction a rectangle trunk for each treetop. Write a numeral on the trunk and draw that number of apples on the treetop. Do not attach the treetops and trunks. Put the treetops and trunks in the center of your circle and let the students take turns matching the trunks to the treetops with that many apples. *Variation:* Cut apples out of red paper (or use dried lima beans painted red). Have the students count out the correct number of apples to match the number on the trunk of each tree.

*Pin the Leaf on the Tree:* Cut a large, brown trunk and a green treetop out of construction paper. Hang it on a wall or bulletin board. Cut out individual leaves for each student. If it is fall, use red, orange, and yellow paper for the individual leaves. Blindfold students as they tape the leaves to the tree. It is fun to see where the leaves end up. There is no wrong place for a leaf in this game. Count the leaves when they are on the tree.

## Art . . . . . . . . . . . . . . . . . . . . . . . . . . . . . . . . . . . . . . . . . . . . . . .

*Leaf Windows:* Go on a nature walk and ask the children to collect a variety of leaves. This is best in the fall when the leaves are colorful. Iron three pretty or unusual leaves between two sheets of wax paper. Cut the wax paper in a decorative shape around the leaves and hang in the window.

*Bark Rubbings:* Take paper and crayons outside to do bark rubbings. Place the paper against the bark and rub with the flat of the crayon on the paper. Turn the paper on different angles and use different colors of crayon to fill up the paper to make a bark collage.

## Food . . . . . . . . . . . . . . . . . . . . . . . . . . . . . . . . . . . . . . . . . . . . . .

Make "Dirt" for pretzel trees to grow in.

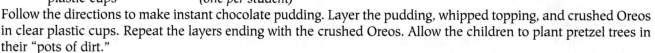

    Ingredients:

| | |
|---|---|
| chocolate pudding | *(mix and milk)* |
| Oreos | *(chocolate sandwich cookies)* |
| Cool Whip | *(whipped dessert topping)* |
| pretzel rods | *(one per student)* |
| plastic cups | *(one per student)* |

Follow the directions to make instant chocolate pudding. Layer the pudding, whipped topping, and crushed Oreos in clear plastic cups. Repeat the layers ending with the crushed Oreos. Allow the children to plant pretzel trees in their "pots of dirt."

To make trees, use the pattern below to cut out green construction paper treetops. Cut a strip of green paper for each tree (3 cm x 8 cm). Tape or glue the paper strip onto the back of the treetop around the end of the pretzel.

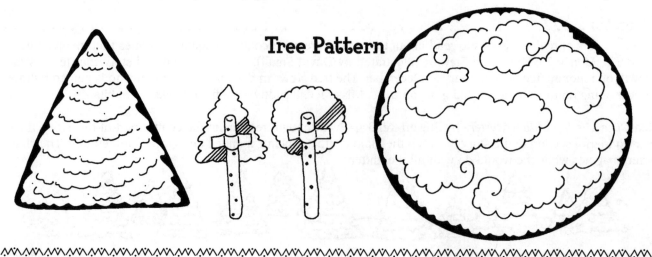

**Tree Pattern**

∧∧∧∧∧∧∧∧∧∧∧∧∧∧∧∧∧∧∧∧∧∧∧∧∧∧∧∧∧∧∧∧∧∧∧∧∧∧∧∧∧∧∧∧∧∧∧∧∧∧∧∧

# Vegetables and Fruit

## Building Language Experience

Ask the children to name their favorite vegetables and fruits. Talk about the different ways that they are prepared. Most vegetables and fruits can be eaten raw or cooked. Talk about the importance of eating vegetables and fruits every day. Vitamins and minerals keep you healthy. Different fruits and vegetables provide different vitamins and minerals, so it is important to eat a variety of foods.

Talk about the different ways that fruits and vegetables grow: on trees, bushes, plants, and underground. Can the students recall how their favorite fruits and vegetables grow? It is helpful to have pictures of fruit trees and vegetable gardens for this discussion.

## Senses

Bring in a variety of produce, especially some less familiar ones. Feel and talk about the different textures. Smell the fruits through the skin and after they are cut. Does the smell change? Do vegetables smell as strongly as fruits? Compare the colors of the fruits and vegetables. Sort them into groups of similar colors. Why are they different colors? After washing the foods, allow the children to taste some of them. Discuss and sort the flavors in terms of sweet, salty, bitter, or sour. Discuss the importance of trying new foods.

## Literature

Read *The Very Hungry Caterpillar* by Eric Carle. Ask the children to name the foods that the caterpillar ate that were good for him. What foods gave him a stomach ache? Obtain a large cardboard box. Cut a child-size hole in each side (at least four sides) Paint a different food from the story around each hole (apple, strawberry, plum, orange, etc.) The students may crawl through the holes in the cardboard box as if they were the caterpillar eating that food.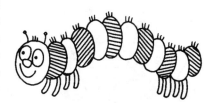

## Games

***Vegetable and Fruit Relay:*** Divide the class into two to four teams. Give each team a large spoon and a variety of vegetables and fruits, such as a banana, carrot, apple, onion, and kiwi. (Each group should get the same number and type.) The first person in each team must carry one fruit or vegetable on the spoon across the room and place it in a basket. If the food falls or if the carrier touches it, he or she must go back and start again. When the food is in the basket, the first player brings the spoon to the second player who chooses a different fruit or vegetable to carry across the room on the spoon. The team that carries all their fruits and vegetables across the room first is the winner. Try out your spoons with all the foods to make sure it is possible before expecting the children to do it.

***Vegetable and Fruit Riddles:*** Give a clue about a specific fruit or vegetable. The children may ask questions and guess what it is. For example, "I'm thinking of a fruit with a furry brown skin that is green and black inside. What is it?" (kiwi)

## Cognitive Skills

Put a tub of potting soil in the center of the circle. Purchase a couple bunches of carrots with tops so that you have at least ten carrots. Hold up number cards (one at a time) and allow the students to take turns planting or removing carrots from the soil in order to have the given number of carrots planted in the soil. Provide garden gloves. Put plenty of newspaper under the tub to prevent a mess. Put the materials in a center for children to explore on their own later.

*Order of Size:* Cut a carrot into about eight round slices. Put the slices in a resealable bag. Students take the carrots out of the bag and put them in order from smallest to largest.

*Patterns:* Duplicate at least four copies of page 75 and cut apart the vegetable and fruit cards. Glue the cards on larger paper so they are easier to hold. Ask four students to stand up where everyone in the circle can see them. Hand them cards in a simple pattern, such as apple, pear, apple, pear. Ask the rest of the class to read the pattern to you and tell you what comes next. Assign other students to come up and add to the pattern by choosing the correct cards and standing with the others. Repeat with other patterns and different students. Choose more difficult patterns according to the ability of your class.

## Creative Dramatics

The children will pretend to eat different fruits and vegetables that you name. Encourage them to act it out from preparation to reacting to the taste. For example, if you name watermelon, they may first carry the heavy melon, cut it into slices, bite the slice, and spit out the seeds. A lemon may produce some wonderful sour faces. You may wish to have half the class act at a time, while the other half observes, then switch for the next food.

## Art

Cut several different vegetables in half. Use the cut side for making vegetable prints. Put paint on a paper plate. Dip the cut side of a vegetable in the paint. Stamp the extra paint off on the plate before stamping on a sheet of paper. Use paint colors to match the vegetable colors: orange for carrots, purple for eggplant, white for onion, brown for potato, etc.

## Field Trip

Visit the grocery store to see a large variety of fruits and vegetables. If you arrange a tour, they will show the children how they preserve and prepare the food.

## Dismissal to the Next Activity

Dismiss children to the next activity by naming their favorite vegetables. For example, if your favorite vegetable is carrots, you may go to housekeeping.

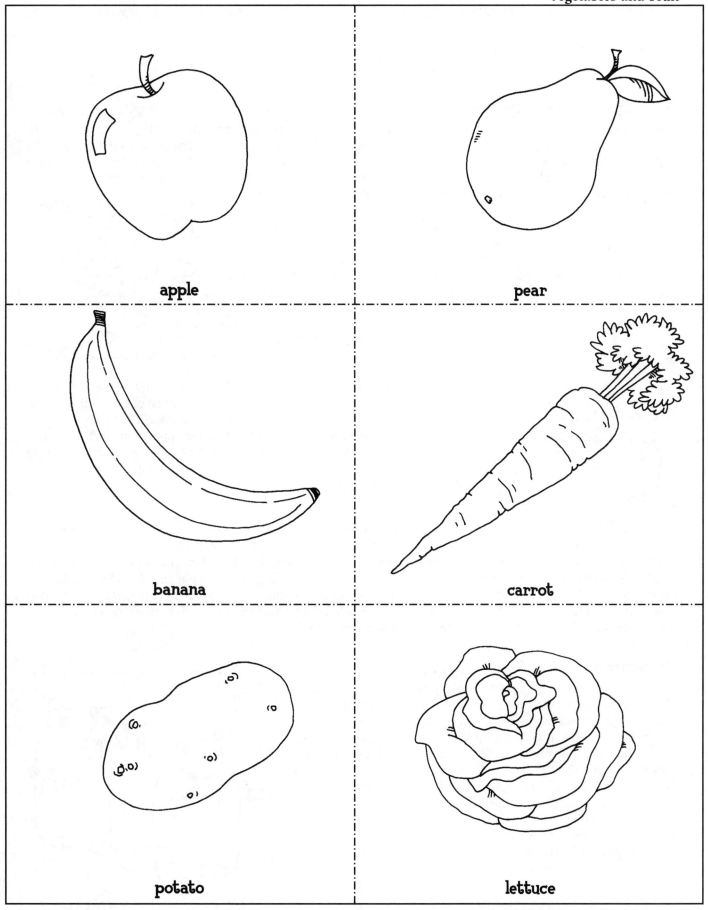

apple

pear

banana

carrot

potato

lettuce

# Water

## Building Language Experience .................................................

Ask students to talk about all the uses of water (drinking, cooking, bathing, swimming, boating, home for animals, watering plants, rain, squirt guns, sprinklers, washing clothes and dishes, etc.). Tell the students that most of the water on earth is salt water that we cannot drink. Of the water that is fresh, much of it is polluted. Water is such an important resource to us; it is essential that we work to keep it clean. Talk about ways that water gets polluted. Ask children to think of things they can do to reduce water pollution.

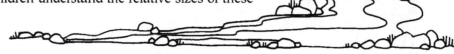

How many different bodies of water can you name? Talk about ways that we find water in nature: ponds, streams, creeks, rivers, lakes, puddles, oceans, waterfalls, swamps, and so on. Listen to children's experiences with those places. Also discuss proper names of these places: Atlantic Ocean, Lake Michigan, Mississippi River, and so on. It is helpful to have maps and photos to help children understand the relative sizes of these different bodies of water.

## Creative Dramatics .................................................

Water is useful for so many things. Have each child take a turn acting out one way we use water. The other children must guess what the child is doing with water. You can let the children think of their own actions or whisper to them something to act out. Some suggestions include brushing teeth, fishing, washing dishes, swimming, rowing, wading, washing hands, drinking, playing in the sprinkler, taking a bath, watering a plant, and stomping in puddles.

## Classifying .................................................

Discuss animals that live in water. Some animals live under the water all the time. Some animals live in the water but breathe the air. Some animals like to swim and bathe in the water but don't live in it. Other animals do not want to go in the water at all! Duplicate page 78 and cut apart. On a large sheet of paper, color a blue pond with grass around it. (Or cut a pond out of blue construction paper and glue it on a large sheet of green construction paper.) As you pick up one of the animals from page 78, talk about where the animal lives in relation to the water. As you discuss, place the animals on the paper where they best fit.

## Cognitive and Music Skills .................................................

Collect as many as seven glass bottles or jars (of similar shape and size). Remove the labels and fill the bottles with graduated levels of water to make a water xylophone. Set up the bottles on a tray in any order. Put the bottles in the middle of the circle along with different tools and utensils for mallets (metal spoon, knife, and fork; plastic utensil; wooden mallet; stick; pencil; etc.). Demonstrate how to tap the side gently to produce a sound. Allow the students to take turns tapping with different utensils on different bottles. Talk about the different sounds. Lead the children to discover that different amounts of water produce different sounds. Ask them to help you put the bottles in order from lowest to highest.

## Exploring the Senses

Clean out several empty soda-pop bottles with caps. Put different things in the bottles for students to observe and swirl around. In one bottle, add water with a light corn syrup and food coloring. In another, fill halfway with colored water and half with baby oil. In another, add water and colored cellophane pieces. In any of the bottles, put materials to add color and interest: pieces of curling ribbon, marbles, confetti, or glitter. Pass the bottles around and discuss with the children what they hear and see as they swirl the contents around.

## Science

Make ice with water and food coloring. Do different things with the ice. Put some colored ice in two bags. Let one melt in the sun and the other in the shade. Predict and watch which one melts faster. Put colored ice in a clear glass of water and watch the colors mix. Notice that the condensation on the outside of the glass is not colored. The reason for this is because condensation comes from the air in the room. It does not leak through the glass.

*Water Table:* Set up a water table for children. Provide floating and sinking objects, as well as pouring and sifting containers. Set towels around the area and have children wear waterproof smocks while playing. On another day, put lots of ice cubes in a tub of water. Give the students tools for fishing the cubes out of the water: tongs, slotted spoons, shovels, metal spoons, plastic spoons, forks, and small cups. Provide a clean pail for ice cubes. Students can dump the ice cubes back in when their turn is over.

## Art

With a wet sponge, get a sheet of drawing paper wet. Have the children use chalk or pastels to draw a picture on the wet paper.

Color a pond scene with crayons. Color the water with blue and green markers. Dip the finished paper in a tub of water. Let it dry on newspapers.

# Animal Patterns
Directions found on page 76.

# Weather

## Building Language Experience

Draw different weather symbols (sun, clouds, raindrops, snowflakes). Cut them apart. Talk about each symbol and how it describes a certain type of weather. When the sun is out, what does it feel like? What clothes do we wear? What do we call that kind of day? (sunny) How do you feel when we have a sunny day? Repeat with the other weather symbols. Decide what kind of day it is today and pin that symbol by the calendar. Put the other symbols nearby so you can talk about the weather each day.

Blow up a balloon in front of the children. Hold the balloon up in front of the class and ask them what is inside the balloon. They will probably say air. Ask them how they know there is air in the balloon. They may say that they saw you blow it in the balloon or that the shape of the balloon tells them that there is air in it. Slowly release the air so it blows your hair or something light as evidence that there is air in it. Ask the children where else they see evidence of the air around them. (flags blowing, leaves moving, sailboat, feel the breeze on their skin, etc.) Tell them that weather is made by the air, sun, and water.

## Literature

Read *Cloudy with a Chance of Meatballs* by Judi Barrett. This very funny book is about a town that has unusual weather. Each day, the citizens of the town watch the weather report to learn what they will be EATING that day. It is a fun idea until one day something goes wrong.

## Finger Play (Mother Goose Rhyme)

| | |
|---|---|
| Rain on the green grass, | *(flutter fingers by the ground)* |
| And rain on the tree, | *(stand up straight with arms like branches)* |
| And rain on the housetop, | *(hands form point of a roof)* |
| But not on me! | *(point at yourself)* |

## Science

Make a rainy environment in a jar. Use an empty spaghetti sauce jar and an aluminum pie tin full of ice. Pour about a cup of boiling water (from a thermos) into the jar. Quickly cover with the pan full of ice. (If possible, turn out the light and shine a flashlight in the jar.) As you observe the jar, ask the children to describe what is happening. You should see the inside of the jar filling up with a cloud and drips of water. The bottom of the pan will become heavy with water. Ask the children where that water is coming from. Some children will probably think it is leaking through the lid. (You don't need to introduce the word condensation— just provide the experience.) Ask them if they have ever seen anything like this anywhere else.

⋀⋁⋀⋁⋀⋁⋀⋁⋀⋁⋀⋁⋀⋁⋀⋁⋀⋁⋀⋁⋀⋁⋀⋁⋀⋁⋀⋁⋀⋁⋀⋁⋀⋁⋀⋁⋀⋁⋀⋁⋀⋁⋀

## Cognitive Skills Games . . . . . . . . . . . . . . . . . . . . . . . . . . . . . . . . . .

*Which Weather?* Draw weather symbols on construction paper. Choose four to six children to stand in front of the class. Each child will hold a weather symbol. The other children look at them carefully and try to remember in what order the weather symbols are arranged. The weather children step out of the room and mix up their order. When they come in again, the other children take turns trying to put them back in their original order. Repeat with different children in a different order.

*Make a Rainstorm:* While sitting cross-legged in the circle, have the children imitate what you do to create the sound of a rainstorm gradually building up and then slowing down again. Discourage the children from talking. Encourage them to just listen and imagine they are making the sounds of a rainstorm.
Slowly rub your hands together.
Snap your fingers with any students who can snap.
The others keep rubbing their hands.
Then slap your legs with your hands.
Now stomp your feet and slap your legs at the same time *(or alternately).*
Just slap your legs with your hands.
Then snap your fingers.
Then rub your hands together.
Now stop and listen to the quiet.

## Food . . . . . . . . . . . . . . . . . . . . . . . . . . . . . . . . . . . . . . . . . . . . . . . . . . .

Make Blueberries in the Snow:
Ingredients:
graham cracker crust
1 pkg. Dream Whip (prepare according to directions)
2 cups powdered sugar
8 oz. softened cream cheese
2 tsp. vanilla
can of blueberry (or cherry) pie filling

Make Dream Whip according to package directions. Mix powdered sugar, cream cheese, vanilla and Dream Whip together and put into crust. Top with fruit filling. Chill before serving.

⋀⋁⋀⋁⋀⋁⋀⋁⋀⋁⋀⋁⋀⋁⋀⋁⋀⋁⋀⋁⋀⋁⋀⋁⋀⋁⋀⋁⋀⋁⋀⋁⋀⋁⋀⋁⋀⋁⋀⋁⋀⋁⋀